Praise for *BabyCalm*™

"Sarah Ockwell-Smith's *BabyCalm*™ of advice that so often overwhelm Ockwell-Smith's goal is to help ne instincts, and learn to trust themse she shares her stories and those to consider their own needs and l strategies, from the 'Tiger-in-the-Tree' baby-calming hold, to the suggestions for recovering from a psychologically traumatic birth. But the real treasure in this book is the reassuring, anti-guilt approach, which is why it's perfect for any mother-to-be."

> **—Dr. Laura Markham, Aha! Parenting.com**

"As a first-time mom the ideas contained in the *BabyCalm*™ book make perfect sense and it gave me the confidence and knowledge to enjoy my new family. Faith is a very happy little girl and we are very happy parents."

> **—Michelle Heaton, singer and new mom**

"As a new mom of a colicky baby I found this book and its advice soothing, not only for my baby but for me! It's an essential prebirth read and a valuable reference after birth."

> **—Lucy Speed, actress and new mom**

"Your book is my bible right now."

> **—Zoe Cole, wife to professional dancer Brendan Cole**

"*BabyCalm*™ is a brilliant, positive resource that focuses on intuition, feelings, love, and trust."

> **—Sheena Byrom, OBE, freelance midwifery advisor**

"Everything . . . in the book really resonated with the way we hoped we would parent."

> **—Dame Sarah Storey, British paralympian**

BABYCALM

BabyCalm™
calmer babies & happier parents

A Guide for Parents on
Sleep Techniques,
Feeding Schedules, and
Bonding with Your New Baby

Sarah Ockwell-Smith

Skyhorse Publishing

Visit our website at www.skyhorsepublishing.com.

10 9 8 7 6 5 4 3 2 1

Library of Congress Cataloging-in-Publication Data
Ockwell-Smith, Sarah.
Babycalm : a guide for parents on sleep techniques, feeding schedules, and bonding with your new baby / Sarah Ockwell-Smith.
pages cm
Summary: "Congratulations! You are about to become, or recently became, a new mom. But now what? You may feel overwhelmed by all the advice given to you by friends, family members, online sites, and the slew of contradicting information about calming a crying baby, getting on a feeding schedule, and training your infant to sleep through the night. BabyCalm[trademark symbol] (a company founded in 2007 in England by Sarah Ockwell-Smith and expanding to the United States this year) runs classes that aim to turn stressed-out parents and crying babies into happier parents and calmer babies. In BabyCalm[trademark symbol], Ockwell-Smith sets out to provide new mothers with the inspiring ethos and methods of her successful company. BabyCalm[trademark symbol] aims to empower new parents to raise their baby with confidence. Focused primarily for new mothers (but with a plethora of sound advice for fathers as well), Ockwell-Smith provides a wealth of information-starting with trusting your maternal instincts above all else-on calming your crying baby, implementing sleep training techniques, facilitating a feeding schedule, bonding with your new infant, understanding your baby's essential needs, and much more. Including parenting tips from around the world as well as ways in which to create confident children, BabyCalm[trademark symbol] is the only book you'll need to set you on the solid path of good (and stress-free) parenting during your baby's first year. "-- Provided by publisher.
Summary: "A guide for new mothers (and fathers) about how to best calm their babies so the whole family is happier and better rested"-- Provided by publisher.
ISBN 978-1-62873-670-0 (pbk.)
1. Infants. 2. Infants--Care for. 3. Parent and infant. 4. Parenting. I. Title.
HQ774.0325 2014
649'.122--dc23
2013035874

Printed in the United States of America

About the Author

Sarah Ockwell-Smith graduated from university with a Bachelor of Science degree in psychology, before spending several years working in pharmaceutical research and development. Following the birth of her first child, Sarah re-trained as a pediatric homeopath, HypnoBirthing antenatal teacher, and birth and postnatal doula. She has also undertaken training in baby massage, hypnotherapy, and psychotherapy.

Sarah founded BabyCalm™ in 2007, in response to the many parents who, having worked with her in the run up to their baby's birth, then asked for support and guidance with their newborn. With help from business partner Charlotte Phillips, Sarah has seen BabyCalm™ grow from humble beginnings in her living room to a company with over one hundred teachers in countries as far afield as Australia, Canada, Ireland, and Spain.

During her career Sarah has worked with over one thousand new parents, helping them to prepare for an easier birth experience and calmer "babymoon." She likes nothing more than watching a nervous new mother blossom into a confident, happy mother and feels honored to play a small role in this process.

Sarah is, most importantly, a mother to four young children. She lives with her husband, children, cats, collie, and several chickens in a four-hundred-year-old cottage in rural Essex.

Contents

Acknowledgments

I would like to express my gratitude to all of the parents I have worked with over the years, who have trusted me to help them at a very special time in their lives and taught me so much about babies, parenting, and myself. Particular thanks go to the parents who have shared their stories in this book: Claire-Louise, Kerry, Tracey, Sam, Katie, Charlotte, Rosie, Lisa, Corinne, Alex, Kate, Imogen, Lucy, Katherine, and Sian.

Thank you to those who have taught me so much along the way: Dr. James Demetre, my Developmental Psychology lecturer at the University of Greenwich; Isla Ball, ex-midwife and International Association of Infant Massage teacher, who provided a listening ear and helped me to learn to trust my maternal instincts; Marie Mongan, founder of the HypnoBirthing Institute, for restoring my faith in birth and my body; Dr. Michel Odent, for his amazing insight into the importance of birth and for introducing me to the role of a doula; and Peter Walker, for an inspiring weekend of Developmental Baby Massage and Movement.

A special thanks to my business partner and BabyCalm™ co-director Charlotte Phillips for pulling me out of my comfort zone and being instrumental in bringing the BabyCalm™ Maternal Revolution to the masses and to our BabyCalm™ teachers, a wonderful group of positive, powerful, inspiring mothers who all share our goal and provide so much support to new parents all over the world.

Lastly, thanks go to my family: my incredibly supportive husband, Ian, who has been both dad and mom to our children during my many weekends of teaching and long evenings of writing; to my late parents, Lynda and David, for my happy childhood; and most of all to my four children, Sebastian, Flynn, Rafferty, and Violet, for being my biggest teachers of all.

Foreword

I don't know many parents who feel they know all there is to know about looking after their newborn baby or raising their children. When I gave birth to my first baby in my early twenties I was constantly on the phone asking the advice of my sisters and my mom. Being the youngest of five girls and having a large family network around me I was easily reassured that what I had "guessed" or felt was the right thing to do was indeed a good plan. Phew! But I was lucky—family units are becoming more dispersed and the support and wisdom of family members isn't always readily available.

Even though I had the benefit of wise advice from relatives with first-hand experience, it was the fashion in the 1970s to read a baby guidebook. None of my older sisters had felt the urge to use such a resource, but I was lulled into believing it was the "modern" thing to do. Up until then I was doing fine, trusting my feelings and the suggestions from my siblings and wider family. But the book I read challenged my natural instinct to love and nurture my baby: I can remember feeling uncomfortable and worried about some of the detailed instructions on how to "train" my baby. Unsurprisingly I soon abandoned the book. After that I continued to enjoy my daughter and went on to relish my other three children just as much but with increasing confidence.

I am now a grandmother and could be considered one of the wise older members of the family. I pass on tips when invited to, but I have also learned so much from watching my children parent their little ones too. I have seen the benefits of co-sleeping and marveled at their positive use of slings. And this is why I was delighted and honored to be asked to write the foreword for this book, where the focus is on nurturing, baby-led parenting that empowers the mother—and father—to trust their instincts and enjoy the precious short time they have with their baby.

At a time when women are becoming more and more reliant on health professionals during pregnancy and birth, and on those who claim to be parenting experts in the years to follow, this book offers a refreshing change. *BabyCalm™* is a brilliant, positive resource that focuses on intuition, feelings, love, and trust. Phrases like "you don't need to be an expert to be a mother" and "be led by your baby" make my heart sing. I love the fact that Sarah offers a range of top tips for particular situations, rather than prescriptive instructions, but is clear that as every baby is unique, each of the tips may need to be tried.

Instead of being authoritarian, the language in the book is simple and facilitative, which aids understanding and supports confidence-building. Sarah uses parents' stories to illustrate points, which always brings "real life" to the topics covered in each chapter. The stories are honest and often frank and will help parents to understand that they are not alone in their quest to successfully care for their baby.

For me, one of the best messages in the book is in relation to the work of the British pediatrician Donald Winnicott, who suggests that the best mother is "a good enough mother." This concept makes perfect sense to me—at the birth the mother is led by the baby's needs totally and as time goes on the baby learns to be more independent, essentially as a result of his mother's imperfect ability to fulfill his every need. So being "just good enough" *is* enough because it promotes the baby's development. It certainly takes the pressure off women trying to reach the impossible goal of "perfect mother."

As a midwife of more than three decades, I am an avid supporter of natural and positive childbirth. I have witnessed first-hand both the positive and negative effects of childbirth on women and families. If birth is perceived by the mother as traumatic the repercussions can last for generations, and I have worked with women where this has been a sad reality. The optimum solution to this would be to ensure all women have a fulfilling, positive birth experience that enables them to form a nurturing, loving bond with their newborn. But I believe that if women are supported following a negative event, and resolution is reached, then the mother–infant relationship has the potential to flourish normally. In addition, a book such as *BabyCalm*™ will provide further support and encouragement for the mother to gain confidence in her ability to lovingly care for her baby, despite a less than ideal start.

The mother–infant dyad is the most important relationship in human existence and forms the foundation of our physical, psychological, and social wellbeing. This book encourages natural and intuitive parenting by building on what the mother already knows and guiding with a selection of suggestions and tips. I hope you find it both useful and confidence-building. I will certainly be recommending it through my work and to my family and friends.

—Sheena Byrom, OBE, freelance midwifery advisor

Introduction

Birth is not only about making babies. Birth is about making mothers. Strong, competent, capable mothers who trust themselves and know their inner strength.

—Barbara Katz Rothman, author and professor of sociology

You may be thinking here is yet another book written by the latest "expert" telling parents the dos and don'ts of babycare and promising miracles (usually of the full night's sleep variety) if you follow their routines to the letter. I don't know you and I don't know your baby—how could I possibly tell you what to do? As you read on, I hope you will find this book different and a refreshing contrast to others you may have already read.

My aim with this book is to take you on a journey, which I hope will help you to realize that you are already the best possible expert when it comes to parenting your baby; you don't need routines, you just need to trust in yourself and in your baby. Why is there a need for books telling us how to raise our offspring by sticking to routines anyway? Parenting seems to come so easily, so naturally, to every other species on our planet, so why not to humans? Do such books really help us? If you have read them, did they help you? Or, perhaps, does such "expert" advice keep mothers disempowered?

Is it possible that these books even keep us from discovering our own maternal instincts? Granted, some moms may not feel like they have much maternal instinct and some moms I have met say they felt as though they didn't have any at all. One thing I can categorically tell you is that your maternal instinct may be deeply buried, shy, or hesitant to appear, but I promise you it is there. If you are someone who is worried that you don't have any maternal instinct, one of the most positive things you can do is to take time just to be with your baby, don't worry about tomorrow or your (perceived lack of) abilities at understanding him, just enjoy today, enjoy the cuddles, and embrace the craziness of your new world. You will find, often when you're least expecting it, that your maternal instinct arises. I have never met a mother for whom this hasn't happened eventually. If you push yourself to be a "good mother" you will open yourself up to a whole world of hurt and confusion, and often the journey to awareness and trusting your instinct will take so much longer.

The BabyCalm™ Philosophy

So where did we go wrong? I believe one of the problems is the loss of female support, the great supportive feminine wisdom we once shared with mothers, sisters, aunts, cousins, and friends. Prominent psychoanalyst Daniel Stern, who specializes in infant development, wrote about a new mother's need to form a "maternal matrix," which he described as a network of maternal figures to help her feel validated and supported in her new role.

This is what the BabyCalm™ philosophy is all about: through our network of female teachers, all of whom are mothers themselves, we offer a mix of weekly classes and one-off workshops for new mothers that can be taken during pregnancy up until their babies are six months old. At these classes and workshops our BabyCalm™

teachers help new mothers to understand their baby's needs, cues, and signals. The aim is to help mothers to find ways to calm their baby's cries, build realistic expectations of their babies, and hopefully get a little more sleep. Most importantly of all, though, we provide a safe, nonjudgmental environment for mothers to talk and a place where people really listen. We support, we listen, and we provide non-biased, evidence-based information and foster individual learning and discovery, rather than forcing opinions onto participants. Our main aim at BabyCalm™ is rebuilding that much-needed supportive maternal matrix and beginning to give back the power to mothers to trust their instincts and be their own expert. This, also, is the main aim of this book: support not prescription.

Over the course of my work with new parents I have met many mothers and babies who have taught me so much more than I could ever learn from a textbook or lecture; their experiences are all unique and equally fascinating. I have shared some of their stories with you throughout this book and thank them deeply for taking the time to write them down and agreeing to share them with you. I hope some of the things they say resonate as deeply with you as they did with me.

You Are the Expert!

How, then, do our modern-day, self-proclaimed "baby experts" help new mothers to feel validated and supported? How do they help her to explore the new feelings being generated within her? How do they help her to grow in confidence, to develop trust in her mothering skills? I suppose it is not good business sense for "baby experts" to nurture new mothers to grow in confidence; after all, the longer the mothers remain lacking in confidence, the more they continue to buy the books, join the forums, and call the help lines.

The very idea that a mother needs an external expert to tell her what to do implies that she does not possess the necessary skills herself—and herein lies the problem.

I believe it is time that the mothers of the world unite and squash this global repression of maternal instinct. With nuclear families, who often live far from relations, we may not have the large female support network we once had around us, but there are other options. We need to find our own voice—that voice deep down inside—and we need to learn to trust it. We need to know that it's OK to hold our babies when every cell in our body yearns to hold them close, calming their tears and rocking them to sleep, despite the latest expert telling us to not make a rod for our own back. It's OK to snuggle that sweet, warm, intoxicating-smelling bundle of love into your arms at night; you won't be "spoiling" them forever by not teaching them to "self-settle." It's OK to respond to your baby. It's OK to love them unconditionally. It's OK to be the mom you are. You are the best mom your baby could have. You are "good enough."

If I could help the new mothers in the world to understand just one thing, what would it be? That YOU are the expert! You already know so much more about your baby than you think you do, even if you think you know nothing at all! In fact, you know more than anybody else in the world. You just have to learn to trust and let that knowledge out. May I suggest you start by getting rid of all of those disempowering books with their rigid routines and the techniques that instinctively feel so wrong, because all of the information you need is inside yourself. You just have to find it and that is where this book can help!

This book aims to be different to those written by the baby experts who imply that the only "right" way to raise your baby is to follow their instructions based on their experiences of other people's children. Instead, I hope that this book will give you the information and confidence to trust your instincts as a parent, with your children, your way. It is full of practical tips and advice, not just from me but from lots of other parents too, as well as helpful explanations of why your baby behaves as he does.

If any of the advice doesn't feel right to you, then don't follow it; there is no "right" way when it comes to raising your baby, just the way that feels right for you. All of the information contained in this book is based on sound research rather than anecdotal evidence and I have also included lots of stories of real mothers' experiences with their babies, giving you the reassurance that your baby's behavior is just that—normal baby behavior. Most importantly, this book does not portray childrearing as a battle that must be won; instead, it shows you that you can raise a happy, confident family where everyone's needs are considered and respected.

One of the main aims of BabyCalm™ and this book is to bring about a change in the way we parent and support new parents. The aim is to help mothers realize they are their own best experts and they don't need to follow the advice or routines of "baby experts." We call this the "maternal revolution"—the revolution of giving back power and confidence to mothers all round the world.

My Story

It might help you to understand the position I am speaking from if I introduce myself and give you a little insight into my own experience of new motherhood. Of course I can't possibly understand how you feel, but in many ways I have walked in similar shoes—albeit a different size and style on a very different path.

It was the summer of 2002, the era of the "parenting expert." You either followed Gina Ford's *Contented Little Baby* routine or Tracy Hogg's *Baby Whisperer* "EASY" routine, or a hotchpotch of both. I was on maternity leave from a high-flying career in pharmaceuticals, earning a fantastic salary complete with a large annual bonus, company car, health scheme, cushy pension, and lots of foreign travel. I was ambitious, but most importantly I was in control in a male-dominated world. I had booked a nursery place for when my son was four months old by the time I was 20 weeks pregnant. I was not maternal; in fact, I was the one who hid in the toilets whenever a colleague returned to show off her new baby as I couldn't bear having to hold it and coo in a silly baby voice. I didn't much care for babies beyond window shopping for cute clothing in Baby Gap. I didn't have high expectations of motherhood. I thought babies cried, lots, and I was prepared for stressful days and sleepless nights. I think it's fair to say, however, that I was not prepared for what was about to hit me or how much my life was about to change!

My son, Sebastian, was born on a rainy July day after a very long and traumatic birth. He was the last baby to be born out of my antenatal class and in many ways I was dreading new motherhood, in no small part due to the negative experiences I kept hearing about from others in my class who had already had their babies. Nobody could have been more surprised than me, however, at how deeply and quickly I fell in love and how calm Sebastian was. I seemed to know what he needed to keep him happy and content and it felt great, if a little surreal, that I was seemingly quite good at being a mom, despite my reservations, and actually how enjoyable the experience was. The only problem was that "my way" of doing things didn't fit with the current conventions and I began feeling more and more ostracized from my antenatal group. I loved spending days at home cuddling Sebastian, whereas they all wanted to go to the latest group or class organized to entertain their babies and aid their development.

Sebastian was the last baby of the group, by a long way, to sleep through the night, the last one to have any discernible routine in the day, and definitely the only one who slept in bed with his parents. I remember several occasions where I lied about how hard I was finding the adjustment just so that I would fit in more with the rest of the group and not seem like I was boasting at coffee mornings, yet conversely I felt more and more like a failure when it came to his routines and sleep. In an attempt to fit the mold I bought books by Gina Ford and Tracy Hogg, but I failed at those too. We couldn't achieve a routine and the one night we tried controlled crying ended with me sobbing in a heap outside the nursery door until I could bear it no more and scooped Seb up and brought him back to my bed, feeling wretched that I had inflicted tears and trauma on him in my quest for a perfect sleeping baby. Then I also felt guilty that I was creating a rod for my own back and depriving him of the ability to self-settle. I couldn't win.

What could have been something so wonderful and rewarding led to me feeling inadequate and isolated. I cut ties with my antenatal group, retreated from friends and relatives, and spent hours on the internet seeking support from virtual friends. Sometimes that helped, but sometimes it heightened my feelings of failure. Looking back now I realize all I really wanted was somebody to say "Well done, Sarah, you're doing a great job," but nobody did. It's so rare we compliment mothers on their mothering skills, isn't it?

I think my feelings were compounded by undiagnosed trauma and quite possibly depression resulting from Sebastian's difficult birth, but again nobody asked me how I was doing, particularly emotionally. I had hoped to have a natural waterbirth, yet instead ended up flat on my back wired up to numerous drips and machines and pumped full of drugs. My notes said I had "failed to progress" and I did indeed feel a failure—a failure at birth and a failure at motherhood. It certainly didn't help when friends and family told me, "It doesn't matter now, at least he's here safely, that's all that matters." How could I say to them, "Well, actually it does matter to me—don't my feelings mean anything?," as that would seem selfish, so I kept it all inside. When this was combined with the turmoil I was feeling in trying to be a "good mom" by following Gina and Tracy, which went against every cell in my entire being, it made for a very unhappy first few months.

As time went by I learned to listen more to myself and to Sebastian. I learned that the experts didn't know me or my son, so how could they possibly know what was best for us? I read some truly wonderful books, such as *The Continuum Concept* by Jean Liedloff, that affirmed what my heart was telling me: it was OK to respond to my baby; it was OK to pick him up; I wasn't spoiling him or letting him manipulate me; in actual fact I might well be helping him. Oh, what a blessed relief it was to finally learn to trust in myself and in my baby. From there on motherhood became the most rewarding thing I have ever done; bringing up my baby was the most special job in the world. I decided not to return to my previous career and, slowly, organically, a new path began to appear ahead of me, one I never thought I would ever follow, but one that I am so very grateful for. I hope so much that this book can help you to experience motherhood as I finally saw it—enjoyable, fulfilling, and happy, because a happy mom and a calm baby go hand in hand. In the quest for a calm baby, never forget how important YOU are!

Chapter 1

Trusting Your Maternal Instinct

A mother understands what a child does not say.

Jewish proverb

Do you sometimes feel that you just don't understand your baby? Have you ever been frustrated at not understanding what he wants from you when he cries? I'm sure that these thoughts cross the minds of most new parents—goodness knows they certainly did mine! I promise you, however, that you already know so much more than you think you know. As the American author Joseph Chilton Pearce, who has spent over fifty years researching the human mind and particularly the development of children, says, "Women have millions of years of genetically-encoded intelligences, intuitions, capacities, knowledges, powers, and cellular knowings of exactly what to do with the infant."

Do What You Feel Is Right

My main aim with this book is not to tell you "how to" parent, rather I hope that the stories and information here will help you to realize how knowledgeable you already are and to trust that you know more about your baby than anyone else in the world. This in turn will help you to know that you don't need to follow anybody else's routines or techniques in order to have a calm and contented baby. Right now this might seem impossible, but hopefully one day, not so far away, you will have the confidence to ignore a piece of well-meant advice or comment concerning your baby and go with your gut instinct, your maternal instinct—the very best teacher of all. This idea is beautifully summed up by Hygeia Lee Halfmoon in her book *Primal Mothering in a Modern World*: "Instincts of women are alive nonetheless. One layer at a time, we find ourselves again and, in doing so, we will put humanity back on track. We will once again be free to be our true selves, teachers of love to a species so easily led astray."

What happens if you don't seem to possess this much revered "maternal instinct"? Is there something wrong with you? How will you ever begin to understand your baby half as much as the other mothers who appear to know what their baby needs instantly? And what if you admit to not really enjoying motherhood? That seems to be the cardinal sin to commit as a new mother, doesn't it? Be reassured that these feelings are totally normal and really very, very common: often mothers won't admit that they struggle sometimes, but the vast majority do, and certainly all of these negative thoughts crossed my mind as a new mother.

Skin-to-Skin Contact

Remember that I mentioned earlier how the best way to begin to learn to understand your baby and yourself as a mother is to forget the future, forget the past, ignore the advice, and "just be." Enjoy the sweet moments, the warm cuddles, the wonky smiles, the milk-drunk eyes, the smell of your baby's head, the softness of his skin, and don't pressure yourself to do or be anything else. Enjoy your "babymoon," because it is through these magic golden moments of bonding that understanding and instinct grows. The more you hold your baby skin to skin, the more oxytocin—the maternal love hormone—you will secrete, and the more you immerse yourself in the world of your baby the quicker you will begin to understand him. These new mothers found that the skin-to-skin contact provided by baby massage helped them in ways they never would have imagined:

> We went to a baby massage class once a week and I loved it so much as it was one of the very few times when it was just me and my little boy: no cell phone ringing, no front doorbell ringing, no pile of washing screaming at me, and no diapers to change! Just the two of us, as it had been for so many months before. The power of simply touching my baby made me feel so connected to him and reminded me so much of when he was born—naked, relaxed, intimate, and only eyes for each other. I really believe it helped build the strong connection that we have today. It was like taking time out from life.

> Touching and holding my baby skin to skin just felt the natural thing to do and it was the perfect excuse to spend even more time enjoying that contact with my little one. I loved the way she just totally relaxed and how she used to watch me all the way through—a lovely way to connect with each other. It just made the rest of the world go away for a while and really calmed and grounded me too.

Babywearing

Many mothers also find being in close physical contact with their baby by carrying them around in a sling or baby carrier helps them to connect with their baby and understand them in ways they perhaps wouldn't without such contact. There will be much more about what is known as "babywearing" later in the book, but for now here's how these moms found carrying their baby in a sling a great aid to developing their maternal instinct:

Babywearing is one of my favorite things we do with our daughter. The closeness we get from carrying her in a sling just could not be replicated in a pushchair. She is close enough to kiss, feed, communicate with, and to gauge how she's feeling. What else is there?

Babywearing is hormone heaven! I wore my babies like a proud badge that said I AM a mother. I love it, it's the most wondrous experience, and I'm not going to waste a moment of my baby's life away from me.

I wish I'd been brave enough to try babywearing sooner. The instant closeness and bond that it gave me and my baby was so special. I loved stroking and patting her little bottom reminding me of when I carried her inside me and having her so close I could smell and kiss her all day. We were both relaxed and so happy.

Actually, I think carrying my child defines me as a mother. It is at my core.

Don't Compare Yourself With Other Mothers

One thing you must avoid as a new mother is comparing yourself to other mothers. Never, ever judge yourself by others, not least because the chances are they are feeling the very same as you, even though on the surface they may be exuding "uber-natural earth mother goddess" vibes! Comparing yourself to other mothers makes for a slippery slope of rapidly downward spiraling self-confidence. Your baby doesn't compare you to other moms, so you shouldn't either!

Listen To the Voice Inside

So what is this much talked about maternal instinct, does it really exist, and should you listen to it? The answer is that indeed you should, as the little voice inside telling you to pick your baby up when he cries, when all around you tell you he needs to learn to self-settle, and the urgent need to hold your baby close when everyone tells you not to spoil him or make a rod for your own back, is powerful, it is wise, and it is the only expert you will need as a new parent. As the wise Dr. Benjamin Spock said, "I really learned it all from mothers." Yet those mothers reading from his books wouldn't believe it until they read it from the great doctor. Oh, the irony! When we parent by instinct and listen to our babies, most often our babies are calmer and happier, which in turn boosts our confidence as a new mother in a wonderful, never-ending spiral of positivity and love. This is how it should be; this is what we miss out on when we try to "parent by numbers," poring over the latest new craze or parenting manual.

Ask yourself this, why is it that humans are the only species in the world that need parenting help? Why is it that all those other tiny creatures with even tinier brains can birth multiple babies, suckle them all, keep them safe, and raise them into strong, healthy adults, all with no external input?

In a recent survey of one hundred new mothers, BabyCalm™ found that 38 percent felt unconfident as a new mother with 46 percent feeling that they did not receive enough support, particularly from wider society, including the expert health professionals whose role is to help new mothers. The most shocking answer to our survey came in response to the simple question: "Have you ever received advice as a new mother that went against your own instinct?" A staggering 82 percent replied with a "yes" and several felt compelled to expand on their answer with comments such as:

We were under lots of pressure. If my husband and I had not educated ourselves or had our midwife's support, all of the unsolicited advice would have overwhelmed us as new parents and we might have given in.

I was told I was breastfeeding too much, comforting too much, and not leaving him enough at night to "self-settle." I was told instead to just give him Gaviscon, but actually it turned out he had a milk protein allergy.

When my baby was crying uncontrollably I was told it was what babies do and I would get used to it. Apparently I was just sensitive as I was a new mom.

I was told to leave my baby to cry and I didn't want to do that; I just wanted some support.

This statistic suggests that 82 percent of new mothers, including the above, in our sample were undermined in their role by society; 82 percent of new mothers were advised that their feelings were wrong; 82 percent of new mothers felt torn between what their heart was telling them to do versus what their head was thinking. How sad that we continue to repress our most powerful teacher.

Science and Maternal Instinct

Interestingly, science backs up the idea of mother's instinct, but explanations of quite what it is and how it works differ hugely. I am extremely sad that science feels it needs to validate a mother's instinct, and so often when I read of a newly released piece of research my over-riding thought is, "And they needed an expensive study to tell them that?" yet here is the society we live in, a society obsessed with randomized controlled this and peer-reviewed that, where we seem to believe that if there are no double-blinded placebo-controlled trials indicating validity and reliability then something can't possibly be true. It is yet another reflection of how far removed we are from instinct, intuition, and sometimes common sense!

Back to the science bit: there is, as you would expect, a great divide between sides in the nurture and nature debate. In one corner there is the belief that maternal instinct is a process of nature, a genetic imprint you might say, and in the other corner is the belief it is a process of nurture and the result of our environment. Both hypotheses offer compelling evidence, but I believe it is the nurture side that comes out slightly in front with the idea that mothers are somehow soft-wired to respond instinctively to their infants.

Scientists have shown[1] that mothers show a much greater activity than fathers in widespread regions of the brain when they listen to their own baby crying compared to the cries of others' babies. They have even identified specific regions of the brain that are important in maternal behavior and motivation when listening to babies crying, a system the researchers call the "maternal circuitry." Psychologist Dr. Jeffrey Lorberbaum says, "Conventional wisdom has long suggested that mothers are more attuned to infants, especially their own, than are fathers, our studies suggest that this may be true. Mothers may be very attuned to their own infant as they activate widespread brain regions including ancient regions believed to be important in rodent maternal behavior. Fathering behavior may be less hardwired and a more recent evolutionary phenomenon as fathers only activate newer regions of the brain involved in sensory discrimination, cognition, and motor planning in response to cries."

On a continuation of this theme, a team of researchers from Virginia[2] carried out research on rats and found that "'the ability of mothers' brains to change in response to the new needs of motherhood enables them to respond with a richer and more enhanced behavioral repertoire. A first-time mother must engage in much behavior previously unfamiliar to her." Psychologist Dr. Craig Kinsley also examined predatory behavior in female rats, comparing the behavior of rats that had never given birth and rats that were lactating. The rats were temporarily deprived of food and then given crickets. In order to feed, the rats had to capture and kill the crickets while Kinsley's team observed. In the animal world, a heightened ability to capture prey means a decreased amount of time the mother spends away from vulnerable offspring and this decreased window of vulnerability means a lower infant mortality rate. The results of Kinsley's study confirmed this, with the rats that had never given birth taking around 290 seconds to catch the crickets, while the lactating group took only about 70 seconds. Speaking of their findings, Kinsley commented: "The mammalian female brain expresses a great deal of plasticity and creativity in service to, and in support of, reproduction, In other words, mothers are made, not born."

However, anthropologist Professor Sarah Blaffer Hrdy disputes the idea that mothers are made, not born. She has studied primates for more than three decades and believes that the desire of a mother to care for a child depends on her desire to be a mother and the amount of time spent bonding together. Although she concedes that maternal responses exist, she believes they are biologically conditioned, but not true instincts, saying, "A woman who is committed to being a mother will learn to love any baby, whether it's her own or not; a woman not committed to or prepared for being a mother may well not be prepared to love any baby, not even her own."

One Russian study[3] found evidence for maternal instinct in girls at only two years of age. The results of the study found that maternal instinct begins to show during the second year of life where it manifests in the form of playing with dolls, and this behavior, the researchers found, reached a peak at three to five years of age. The researchers found that playing with dolls occurred subconsciously and believe the formation of family orientation is shaped at an early school age.

Intriguingly though, science also suggests that maternal instinct is present during pregnancy, well before the baby is even born. Scientists[4] in Jackson, Mississippi, studied predictions of fetal weight comparing three methods—ultrasound, clinical estimates (palpation by doctors), and maternal instinct. Of these three measures maternal instinct was by far the most accurate, with almost 70 percent of mothers accurately predicting the weight of their baby to within 10 percent of their birth weight. That's impressive.

On a similar theme researchers at the Johns Hopkins University[5] conducted a study in which they asked 104 pregnant women who did not know the sex of their baby to predict the gender. Their results found that women with more than twelve years of education correctly predicted the sex of their babies 71 percent of the time and furthermore the women whose predictions were based on psychological criteria, such as dreams or feelings, were significantly more likely to be correct than those who based their predictions on external indicators such as how they were carrying the baby. It seems science agrees that mothers do possess an instinct. If only the mothers themselves would believe it!

Worries about Maternal Instinct

In my work with new mothers I come across two main worries when it comes to the topic of maternal instinct.

First, there are the mothers who are advised to ignore their maternal instincts and parent in a way they have been advised is supposedly superior and are struggling, daily, with the inner conflict. Second, there are the mothers who don't think they have any maternal instinct and don't understand their babies.

I believe the root of these worries is threefold: first, mothers receive too much advice from others to ignore their own instincts; second, as a society we do not provide new mothers with the support they really need; and third, we do not value motherhood enough. All three factors combined lead to new mothers often feeling unconfident and insecure in their new role, so they seek to rectify this by educating themselves—and yet the education they receive serves only to undermine their confidence and instincts even more. It is a vicious circle of disempowerment fuelled, ironically, by a need to be empowered.

The Answer

To me, the answer to such worries about maternal instinct (or perceived lack of it) is simple: throw away the more prescriptive baby books and support new mothers, not by taking the baby so they can rest, but by cooking and cleaning for them, telling them how well they are doing, listening to their fears, worries, excitement, and happiness, without giving advice or judgment, and understanding what an amazing job mothers do. We need to stop seeing motherhood as a second-class occupation. How do "stay-at-home" mothers feel when they have to enter their occupation as "housewife" on an application form? Mothers are clever, mothers are wise, mothers are busy, and they do so much even though they may often think they do so little.

As Naomi Stadlen quotes in her book *How Mothers Love*: "It takes time to learn about a baby. It's an extraordinary process. Mothers are learning about hitherto unknown persons. The earliest discoveries they make are often small and imperceptible. A mother might not realise that she is making any progress." She goes on to say: "These mothers have all read books on babycare. But the books are about babies in general. It is different when a mother considers her own baby together with her own ideals and aspirations. She is alone on her unique path. It can feel frightening to admit that she does not know the way ahead. Yet this seems a valuable beginning to being a mother. It enables her to start from a position of humility, from humility it is easier to learn."

Finally, we need to listen to our hearts more and follow our heads less when parenting and, most importantly of all, listen to our babies, for they are the key to unlocking our instinct. As the famous dog trainer (yes, a dog trainer!) Cesar Millan says in *Be the Pack Leader*, "humans are living our lives out of balance. We are in the process of losing the instinctual side of ourselves that make us animal first and human second. And instinct equals common sense. . . . We are masters of reason and logic. We communicate with one another almost exclusively through language. We send worded messages on the internet and cell phones; we read; we watch television. We have lots of education and more information at our fingertips than ever before, which allows some of us to live almost 100 percent in our minds. We agonize about the past and fantasize about the future. All too often, we become so dependent on our intellectual sides that we forget there is much, much more to this amazing world we live in. . . . The good news is our instinctual selves are lying deep within us, just waiting to be rediscovered."

So what if? . . . What if we trusted our babies? What if we looked deep into those baby blues and asked our infants what they needed? What if we learned to trust that—just as Cesar says— "our instinctual selves are lying deep within us, just waiting to be rediscovered"? How would that change the way we parent? What if we ourselves were parented more instinctively; would that change carry on down the generations? Are you a part of changing the future of our race? What a change it would make.

Many of the mothers I meet in my work have commented on how they have learned to trust their instincts and be their own expert, yet the following story always comes to my mind when thinking of maternal instinct. Claire-Louise's story is one I recount time and again when training new BabyCalm™ teachers, and I will look in more detail at many of the subjects she mentions throughout this book.

Claire-Louise is English and her partner is Egyptian. I still remember vividly the day we chatted about her profound experiences as a mother in Egypt compared to life in England.

Claire-Louise's Story

I had quite a lot of experience with babies and children growing up and worked as a nanny for some time in my early twenties. The practical side of taking care of a baby, therefore, was something that didn't faze me. In fact, like most people (seemingly whether they have experience and/or background knowledge or not!), I had quite well-formed opinions about what was "right" and "wrong" in parenting. So much so that when I went to live abroad, first in Madrid, then in Dubai, and later Egypt, I was quite put out that babies and young children were up late at night, out in restaurants or public places with their parents. Surely they should be in bed by now? This was the time parents were supposed to reserve for themselves. Children went to bed around 7 PM and slept until 7 AM. Didn't they?

This more "relaxed" style of parenting bothered me and I felt sure these parents had missed something. One thing I did love, however, was the greater sense of "community" I felt—the feeling of big, open families spending lots of time together; three or four generations enjoying each other's company. Did we have it right after all? Was our "Western" way of living better for society . . . or was "progress" seriously affecting social order? Looking back, these were the seeds of thought that eventually led me to the parenting style I consciously chose when I fell pregnant with my daughter: trusting my instincts, not what was expected of me.

While researching and reading during my pregnancy, I came across the concept of attachment parenting and everything clicked into place. In one sense it seemed ridiculous that I should need to read about trusting my own instincts and going back to the basics when it came to meeting the simple needs of an infant; love, touch, and dependency, even before nutrition. On the other hand, the values and ideas I had grown up with were so ingrained that I had never before questioned whether they were, in fact, "best." Independence in particular was something so strived for in our society, that the thought of letting even a helpless infant thrive in the safe, dependable arms of their mother, was unthinkable. Babies should be encouraged to be independent as early as possible.

I remember the first time I went to my brother-in-law's house in Egypt and saw that his one-year-old daughter slept in the room with her parents. They had some kind of co-sleeper attached to their bed; it was the first time I'd seen anything like it. Of course at the time I thought that was a BIG mistake. I'm sure the comment I made to my husband was along the lines of the "rod for your own back" mantra. Later, when I started talking to my husband about all the "new, exciting" ideas I'd discovered with regards to attachment parenting, he was noticeably unfazed. All the "revelations" I was having were things he had never questioned. Co-sleeping (of course they don't use that name, it's just what they do!), believing in and responding appropriately to our babies' needs/cries, and understanding that the needs were just that at this stage: needs not wants were not news to him. Of course you picked up a baby when they cried. Why would you put them to sleep in a separate room? What do you mean the baby would try to manipulate you with their demands? (He found that one particularly funny when I explained that's what so many people thought!)

I was breastfed for six months and always knew I wanted to breastfeed my own children "if I could." Well, why wouldn't I be able to? Of course, I know there are a small percentage of women who truly can't breastfeed for whatever reason (excluding those who choose not to), but why are we so resigned to thinking we won't be able to? It's a very small minority, not the majority, who can't breastfeed. In Egypt, by contrast, breastfeeding was not something anyone discussed; it was simply the normal way all mothers fed their infants. I now know that this is not only influenced by necessity (cost for example), but also by religion (the Quran talks about feeding an infant for at least the first two years). The most important deciding factor for a new mother, however, was purely that breastfeeding was how their mothers/grandmothers/sisters/aunts/cousins/neighbors, etc. fed their infants. It was normal.

Unfortunately my husband was stuck in Egypt and couldn't be at our daughter's birth. So when she was three weeks old, I took her over to meet her Baba for the first time. We stayed with the family and needless to say not one person asked me if she was "good," or "sleeping through the night yet." There were plenty of women giving me tips on breastfeeding, not one of them mentioning lack of milk, topping up, or dream feeding [a late feed without arousing the baby] with a bottle to "get her to sleep through." Ultimately, it seems, whether you are a new mother in

Egypt, England, or anywhere else in the world, you are vulnerable and sensitive in the first weeks and months, and even well-meaning advice given at the wrong moment can be upsetting. There are always pressures, whether from society, family, the media, or your circumstances. As with everything, it comes back to finding the right balance for you and knowing when to trust yourself and when to seek support and encouragement.

Perhaps the most poignant difference I noticed in Egypt was in the value of mothers, who are hugely respected out there, and where the role of motherhood is seen as the making of a woman, rather than the breaking of her career. I, for one, feel honored and extremely privileged to be blessed with a child to nurture, love, protect, and care for as only a mother can.

Chapter 2

Understanding Your Baby's Needs

In spite of the six thousand manuals on child raising in the bookstores, child raising is still a dark continent and no one really knows anything. You just need a lot of love and luck —and, of course, courage.

Bill Cosby, actor and author

What Do You Think Babies Need?

If you listen to modern society, babies need a long list of equipment, expensive gadgets, items of furniture, an all-singing all-dancing stroller, stimulating toys, educational DVDs, cuddly animals that play a variety of electronic lullabies, and a myriad of different outfits, not to mention the different lotions and potions promising softer skin and better sleep. For many women their worth as a "good mother" is directly linked to how much it has cost to accessorize the nursery. I am guilty of this, having spent £1,000 (roughly $1,500) on a handmade cot-bed for my firstborn: I got caught up in the commercial frenzy and shopped until I dropped, or rather until the credit card reached its limit! A 2011 survey in the United States, conducted by the Bump's Annual Pregnancy and Baby Study, found that new parents spent an average of $4,294 in the first year alone!

Yet, what a baby really needs is so much simpler. Our babies need food; our babies need warmth and shelter. Our babies need us—they are conscious, thinking, feeling tiny little beings, just like us! Their needs are so simple, yet so misunderstood. Psychologist David Chamberlain, a pioneer in birth psychology, says,[6] "Newborn babies have been trying for centuries to convince us they are, like the rest of us, sensing, feeling, thinking human beings. Struggling against thousands of years of ignorant supposition that newborns are partly human, sub-human, or not-yet human . . . Old ideas are bound to die under the sheer weight of new evidence, but not before millions of babies suffer unnecessarily because their parents and their doctors do not know they are fully human."

The World Inside You

Think back to when your baby was inside you, at the very end of your pregnancy, and imagine what his environment was like. Naturally it would have been wet and warm; more importantly the temperature was consistent—he never knew what it was like to be cold or hot until the day of his birth. Everything he touched in his time tucked inside you was soft and warm, whether he was touching himself, the walls of your uterus, or his placenta; it was always soft and warm. He did not know what it was like to have cold plastic or metal on his skin, or rough fabric rubbing him, until the day he was born.

Inside you he was naked; imagine how strange it must feel to wear clothes. How frustrating it must be to try to suck his fist, only to find a scratch mitt on his hand and fabric in his mouth. Inside you he did not experience the weighty effects of gravity, as in his watery world he could swirl around freely; now the heaviness of his own body renders him so much more immobile than he was not so long ago. Inside you he was exposed to constant noise, the sound of your heartbeat, the swish of blood through the umbilical cord, the rumbling of your tummy digesting your food, the hum of your voice. The sound inside the womb was constant and unchanging, and now he must transition to a world that is both deafeningly loud and deafeningly quiet; so many new sounds to take in and yet his reassuring constant noise disappeared the moment he was born.

Inside you it was dark, and although his eyes would have opened as his birth drew nearer he has never seen as he does now, lights so very bright all around him and smells we may take for granted, but that to him are brand new. Some smells are good and reassuring to babies, like the smell of you, the smell of your sweat, the smell of your milk if you are breastfeeding, while some are less so, such as the scent of perfume, shower gel, air freshener, fabric softener, and more.

Last, but by no means least, for this is perhaps the most important point of all, when your baby was inside your uterus he was in physical contact with you, constantly. He was always held, the larger he grew the tighter the resulting hug your uterus gave him, and you were always there. Until his birth he never spent a second away from you. It is small wonder, then, that so many babies like to be held all of the time and only settle in our arms or sleep when next to us. Imagine how your tiny baby must feel to transition from constant physical contact with you to lying alone in a Moses basket within hours of birth.

Several moms I have worked with over the years have commented on the transition for their baby from womb to world and how they found that understanding this enormous change the baby had been through helped them to understand their needs more:

My second baby was very big, 11 lb 2 oz (5kg), and always seemed very uncomfortable and unsettled, especially when he got tired. I really believe it was because he was so used to being incredibly squashed when in utero and it took him a while to get used to being "free." Swaddling helped him to feel secure and to settle to sleep very quickly. It soon became part of our sleep time ritual and he really loved being swaddled.

My baby used to love being in the bath with me. He adored it; floating around almost submersed in the warm water, I imagine it reminded him of life before he was born. He would be so relaxed and calm that when we got out he usually fed and fell asleep on me. Bliss.

In his book *The Diary of an Unborn Child*, Manuel David Coudris attempts to relate to the world of a baby in utero. He writes: "Mama . . . I cannot see you and, therefore, I do not know what you look like, who you are—because I am inside you! I experience my own world, my own feelings. And because you talk to me and I want to receive your voice we have opened the doors to each other and quite deliberately touch one another . . . The inner part of your body, your food, your vibrations, your blood and your bones—your whole body is now my universe."

A Modern Misunderstanding?

We are indeed our baby's universe and we wonder why they cry so much when we try to put them down alone. We wonder why they only sleep soundly when they are in our arms, waking almost as soon as we place them in their cot. We think we should teach them how to "self-settle," we are told never to let a baby fall asleep in our arms, and that they should always be put down awake. To me this is a sad misunderstanding of the needs of babies.

In her 1999 book *The New Contented Little Baby Book,* Gina Ford writes, "By all means cuddle your baby prior to sleep times, but try not to cuddle him to sleep as he may learn the wrong sleep associations and become dependent on a cuddle to get off to sleep . . . Provided your baby is ready to sleep and has been well fed and winded, it is advisable to allow him a short crying down period. Parents who allow their baby to learn how to settle himself in the very early days will very rarely have to go through the procedure of sleep training their baby at a later stage because he has learned all the wrong sleep associations."

Babies, however, need more than a full tummy and their wind removed in order to feel secure enough to sleep; babies also need close physical contact, since to a baby cuddles are as important as food, love is as nourishing as milk to a new baby, and without that contact they fail to thrive.

Research shows that giving your baby what they need at a young age can create a much more stable and psychologically healthy child and adult. As the world-renowned obstetrician and author Dr. Michel Odent says in his book *Primal Health*: "The circumstances of the mother/baby relationship have as much of an effect on the whole culture as the culture has on them. So when the early mother/baby relationship is either helped or hindered, it has consequences for the whole culture." This concept, of attachment and bonding, is so important I have devoted a whole chapter to this very subject later on (see chapter 8).

Babies of Hunter–Gatherers

The realization that society and the modern expert may be wrong is compounded further when we view babies from an evolutionary point of view, particularly if we wind the clock back about 8,000 years and return to our hunter–gatherer roots. Imagine a time over eight millennia ago when the hunter menfolk would go out for many hours hunting for food and the women would gather, foraging for plant-based food. In order to forage all day long the women used to strap their babies onto them, as they could not leave them for long periods of time. The make-up of human breast milk, with its relatively low fat content compared to other mammals and the speed at which it is digested, meant our female forager ancestors could not spend long periods of time away from their babies. Gatherer mothers had to take their babies with them, unlike the menfolk who would spend hours away, or a wolf who would leave her cubs, satiated due to the fatty, slow-digesting wolf milk, for hours while out hunting. Human babies are meant to be with us, it is in our genetic make-up, yet we fight this so much and this fight makes parenting so much harder for us all.

Indeed, recent research by Darcia Narvaez, Professor of Psychology at the University of Notre Dame, Indiana,[7] indicates a link between the style of baby raising prevalent in hunter–gatherer societies and a child's more positive mental health, empathy, conscience development, and intelligence. Professor Narvaez says that "the way we raise our children today in this country is increasingly depriving them of the practices that lead to wellbeing and a moral sense."

William Sears, father of eight children, author of over thirty books on childcare, and Associate Clinical Professor of Pediatrics at the University of California, Irvine, School of Medicine, sums this up quite nicely when he says, "We live in a Western culture which is definitely at odds with this 'primitive' style of mothering. And our babies cry a lot!"

Jean Liedloff, author of *The Continuum Concept*, wrote widely about the needs of babies in relation to her time spent living with the Yequana tribe in the South American jungle. In her article "The Importance of the In Arms Phase," she says, "I came to see that our human nature is not what we have been brought up to believe it is. Babies of the Yequana tribe, far from needing peace and quiet to go to sleep, snoozed blissfully whenever they were tired, while the men, women, or children carrying them danced, ran, walked, shouted, or paddled canoes. . . ." Profound indeed is the notion that we have more to learn from returning to our roots and listening to our instinct and our babies, than we do from science and parenting experts.

As Dr. James McKenna, Professor of Anthropology and Director of the Center for Behavioral Studies of Mother–Infant Sleep at the University of Notre Dame, Indiana, says[8]: "Human infants need constant attention and contact with other human beings because they are unable to look after themselves. Unlike other mammals, they cannot keep themselves warm, move about, or feed themselves until relatively late in life. It is their extreme neurological immaturity at birth and slow maturation that make the mother–infant relationship so important." Perhaps then it is not so hard to understand babies: their needs are simple and they are master communicators if only we really listened to them.

Speaking the Language of Babies

How do we learn the language of babies if this is a new world to us? I wonder if you have come across an experienced mother, your own mother, aunt, or grandmother perhaps, who just knew what your baby wanted and instantly knew how to calm him? I have often been told that I "have a way with babies" and new mothers often say they wish they had my "skills." Here I have to be honest and confess I have no special skills; I do not "speak baby," nor do I possess some magical baby-whispering ability. The only difference may be that I am several years and four children farther down my journey than you are, as a new mother. Also, remember that nobody knows your baby as well as you, even if currently you might not think so.

In my new baby groups I often ask the circle of moms what special noises or movements their babies make that indicated a need to them. Here are some of their replies:

> When he pulls his ear like that I know it's time for his nap, if I don't pay attention and miss his signs he gets cranky and over-tired; if I help him to sleep as soon as I notice it's easy.

> When she wants feeding she does this funny thing with her tongue, putting it in and out quickly like a lizard.

These mothers were the very same ones lamenting their lack of baby understanding just moments before, as for some reason they didn't realize how much communication they were already sharing with their babies!

Just remember, your baby is unique and will have his own unique communication, so the best way to understand him is to really watch and listen to him, and also imagine yourself in his situation. Here are some signs my own babies made and clues I have noticed in other babies: it doesn't mean your baby will do these things and it doesn't mean if he does that he means the same thing, but I hope it will help you to start to notice signs for yourself.

Physical Clues Your Baby May Show

Ear pulling	May mean your baby is getting tired.
Hiccupping	May also mean your baby is getting tired.
Gaze aversion	May mean your baby is tired or over-stimulated.
Pulling up legs	May be just a reflex action when your baby is upset, not necessarily indicating abdominal pain.
Going red	May mean your baby has been crying for too long or is overheated, not necessarily in pain or constipated.
Blue outline to lips	May mean your baby has trapped wind.
Sticking tongue out	May mean your baby is hungry.
Putting fist in mouth	May mean your baby is hungry.

Rooting*	May mean your baby is hungry.
Fidgeting	May mean your baby is hungry.

(*Rooting is a head-turning and sucking reflex towards a stimulus, seen in young babies.)

Sound clues Your Baby May Make

When a baby first starts to cry you can very often notice a difference in the sounds that they make. For instance, a pain cry can sound very different to a tired cry, but once the cry escalates and the baby is lustily screaming it is much harder to work out what is wrong, so understanding your baby's early clues can be hugely helpful. Babies will naturally have their own noises for certain things, which tend to be clearer the older they are, so it is useful to spend some time really listening to your baby to get to know his language.

In her book *Child Sense: How to Speak Your Baby's Language* (2010), Priscilla Dunstan claims that between birth and three months, infants make sound reflexes. According to Dunstan, we all have reflexes, like sneezes, hiccups, and burps, which have a recognizable pattern when sound is added to the reflex. This she calls "Dunstan's baby language."

Developmental Spurts

Just when you think you are beginning to understand your baby, things often go and change. Many parents worry that this is because they have done something wrong but on many occasions it is down to a much more physiological cause. A baby's brain undergoes an enormous amount of development and growth throughout the first year. A newborn's brain is approximately 25 percent of the size of an adult's brain. Your baby's brain is busy making new connections (neural pathways) and your baby is busy learning and changing his perceptions of the world around him. These developmental changes are not immediately obvious to the eye and many new moms wonder what they have done wrong when a baby's sleep regresses or they begin to feed like a newborn again.

At this point we need to go right back to the beginning and realize how scary our world can be for new babies, and that in order to calm a baby we need to understand what they may be feeling. When a baby undergoes a developmental change it is not surprising that he seeks the same comforters as he did in the very early days. As a parent the best thing we can do is understand that the first year in particular is a tremendous time of upheaval for our babies and to give them the comfort they seek in order to proceed through the transitional first year with as little trauma as possible.

Signs a baby may be going through a developmental change can include:

- more frequent feeding
- more frequent night waking
- extra "clingy" behavior
- a fussy and unhappy baby
- a self-settler may need extra help to settle
- daytime nap pattern may change (baby may sleep more or less)
- baby may begin not to like things they previously did.

Common Times for Developmental Spurts in the First Six Months

Age	What May Possibly Be Happening
4 weeks	At this stage babies' vision changes. They can see farther and with more clarity, with the focus

shifting from the corner of the eyes to the center. In particular babies may literally be visually stuck—staring at a particular object but unable to detach their gaze.

8 weeks	Emotional center of the brain really kicks in: babies smile, some may laugh, and are much more aware of their surroundings. They are beginning to make associations (e.g., anticipating food when they see a bottle or breast).
12 weeks	Babies are much more in control of their bodies and may spend a lot of time with their hands in their mouths—this is a normal developmental stage often confused with teething! Frustratingly, though, babies are not always in control, especially when it comes to dropping items they want to let go of!
18 weeks	Babies' understanding of the world is much more advanced and the social center of their brains is really kicking in. However, their bodies are still relatively immature and they are not able to verbalize their feelings. The period of 18 to 24 weeks has long been known to be a time of intense frustration for babies.

In his book *The Wonder Weeks,* Dr. Frans Plooij takes this concept even further, saying, "Our research has shown that from time to time all parents are plagued by a baby who won't stop crying. In fact, we found that, surprisingly, all normal, healthy babies are more tearful, troublesome, demanding, and fussy at the same ages, and when this occurs they may drive the entire household to despair. These changes enable the baby to learn many new skills and should therefore be a reason for celebration." Again the key point here is to empathize with our babies, try to understand what they may be experiencing, and understand why they might need us more during these unsettling periods.

Kerry came to one of my groups in 2009 with her newborn son, Sam. I remember the phone call I had with Kerry when she initially contacted me, as she sounded so sad and spent a good proportion of the call in tears. When she came to the first session she was quiet and withdrawn; her little boy was not at all happy and cried as much as his mother did. It was so upsetting to watch as Kerry clearly adored her baby but was finding it so hard to understand what he needed from her. Of all the mothers I have worked with, I think Kerry is the one who has had the most profound impact on me, and now a mother of two she is so in touch with her children, who are both happy and thriving. Her metamorphosis has been a joy to watch. If you didn't know better you would look at Kerry and think she was "one of those natural mothers to whom everything came easily," but it wasn't always like that.

Kerry's Story

I thought I had prepared myself for having my baby. We'd been to childbirth classes, read the books and magazines, been through the checklist of all the things that you "need" to have. I was lucky enough to have a natural water birth with minimal pain relief, but looking back I think I was still quite traumatized by the experience. Exhausted and totally stressed out with the conflicting advice I was being given by health professionals, the childcare expert books, and well-meaning family, friends, and, on some very unhelpful occasions, total strangers. I felt out of my depth and like I was on a different planet!

Sam was only a couple of weeks old when our health visitor suggested he had colic when I told her that he screamed for about two hours in the evening when we put him down. By the time he was six weeks old he had been on a number of different medications for reflux. I was so glad when I found BabyCalm™ while looking for some support on the internet. I attended the first session as a stressed out, worried wreck, yet even after the first session I felt more calm and confident.

By the end of the course I felt much more confident as a mom, to trust my instincts and my ability to do the right thing for my baby, and to listen to what he was trying to tell me. Learning to babywear* was one of my favorite things and made such a massive impact on our lives. I wish that I had done the course when he was days old not weeks—or even before he was born. I have since had another child and the experience of the first few weeks couldn't have been more different.

(*Babywearing will be examined in much more detail in chapters 3 and 4.)

Chapter 3

A Toolbox of Calming Techniques

Babies are always more trouble than you thought—and more wonderful.

—Charles Osgood, psychologist

When we understand our babies and their world a little more we begin to understand ways in which we can soothe and calm them. The suggestions that follow in this chapter are not rules to be rigorously applied, but ideas to try.

In no way do I intend for this chapter to be a prescriptive list and a "fix all" for all babies. Each and every baby is different and beautifully unique—frustratingly there is no easy equation that equals instant calmness for each and every baby. What one baby loves another may hate and, similarly, what works well for one mother may not be liked by another. The most important thing is that you listen to your baby and your own instinct in order to learn what your baby likes best.

What I have suggested here is a toolbox of commonly used calming techniques for you to try while you and your baby are still learning to communicate with each other (they are in alphabetical order—not in any order of preference):

- babywearing
- deep bathing
- feeding

- movement
- noise
- pacifiers
- skin-to-skin contact
- swaddling
- taking your baby outside
- the tiger-in-the-tree hold.

Babywearing

Wearing your baby in a sling is one of the ultimate ways to keep him calm and happy. It increases the time a baby spends in a state of "quiet alertness"—a time of contentment when he will learn the most. When your baby was in utero he spent 100 percent of his time in physical contact with you—yet the moment he was born this is estimated to drop to only 40 percent. Babywearing also means two free hands, which is very useful indeed for a new parent. It is not surprising that so many of the mothers in my groups rave about it so much and why I also "wore" all four of my babies.

> My eldest had "colic" and in 1984, babywearing was rather a strange thing to do. But I used to put him in the sling (well fed but still screaming) and go and hang out the washing, . . . by the end of the washing line he had relaxed and gone to sleep. . . . it never failed.

> Babywearing saved my sanity. After a C-Section it was painful to carry even a newborn, so I found the support given by the sling invaluable, especially as she would only sleep while being held.

> The sling was the only place she napped for seven months, and the only way I could leave her with her dad as a small baby because it calmed her down so well.

I love babywearing because I can share my world with my son and talk about it with him. We are both happier— even if he was hungry he wouldn't protest until he came out of the sling; he seemed content that he was close to me/milk; close enough to kiss. And sleep! He slept for longer in the sling too, versus 45 minutes at best if he wasn't in contact with me.

The sling was wonderful, like a really long cuddle with no aching arms! Plus it allowed me to breastfeed in public with no embarrassment.

Our sling was a near-instant sleep-inducer for months. He seemed to find it hard to get off to sleep but the sling worked a treat every time.

I'm so glad I discovered babywearing. If I was tired and my baby was upset for whatever reason, I'd pop him in a sling and go for a walk outside, and I found that we would both calm down and get back "into sync" with each other. Plus it meant that no one else could try and pick him up!

If you would like to carry your baby in a sling then do make sure you choose carefully. There are many types of baby carriers available today, some good, some less so. The general rule when searching for a carrier is to find one that is supportive for both your baby and you as the wearer: the sling should not place any strain on your back, neck, or shoulders and similarly should support your baby's back in a physiologically correct convex "C" shape and help support his legs in an "M" shape (or froggy) position so that he remains comfortable and his hips are held in a natural, healthy position. In order to hold your baby in an anatomically correct and comfortable position the carrier needs to support your baby right out to his knees and his knees should

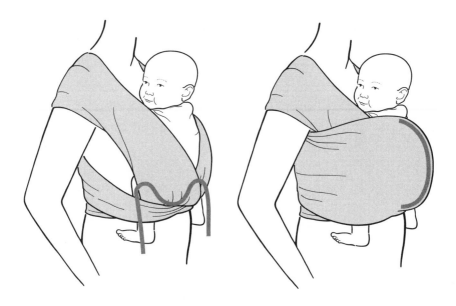

always be higher than his hips. The illustration above left shows the correct "M" position of the baby's hips and legs, while the illustration above right shows the "C" shape you are looking for when the sling is in the final position.

When buying a sling you might want to consider who will be wearing it apart from you, i.e., do you need the sling to be worn by people of different sizes? How long would you like to use the sling for each day? Are you happy to buy a different sling for wearing an older baby or toddler? Or would you just like the sling for the first few months? What position would you like to carry your baby in? What sort of fabric would you like? And would you like a quick "throw it on" sling or would you be happy to use one you have to spend a couple of minutes putting on?

Types of Slings and Baby Carriers

Slings tend to fall into the following categories:

Stretchy Wrap Slings

Stretchy wrap slings are great beginner slings as the stretch in the fabric is very forgiving on the inexperienced babywearer. Wrap slings are long pieces of fabric, usually between 3.5 m and 5.5 m (11 ft 5 in and 18 ft) in length. They can be tied in a variety of positions, which, although on first glance may look very daunting, are actually pretty easy to tie once you've had a bit of practice. Stretchy wrap slings are lovely for newborns and usually support really well until the baby is around six to twelve months of age (depending on the individual baby and sling).

Woven Wrap Slings

Woven wraps have all the advantages of stretchy wraps, plus they are more supportive as the weave of the fabric means they do not stretch with the baby's weight; this does, however, mean they take more practice to fit well. Woven wraps can be used for a multitude of carrying positions, including back carries, and can be used into toddlerdom and beyond. This is the most versatile baby carrier you can buy.

Ring Slings

Ring slings are very easy to put on and do not require any tying. You simply pop it over your head and tighten by pulling the fabric through the rings. Ring slings are generally made out of woven fabric so they can support well and can be used for little babies right into toddlerdom and beyond (when used in a hip carry). They do have a limited range of positions compared to the wrap slings.

Pouch Slings

Pouch slings are very similar to ring slings, but are either fitted to size with no fastenings or they have an adjusting mechanism (such as a clip or fastener). They are very, very quick to put on, but what you gain in speed of use you lose in support. They can be good for short wearing times, such as a quick pop into the supermarket, but they are not supportive enough to wear for long carries. Pouch slings tend to be the cheapest slings to buy but are also the least versatile.

Mei Tais

Mei tais are Asian-inspired carriers. They are similar in style to a wrap sling, with a supportive central panel and then four lengths of fabric off each corner to wraparound and tie. They are usually quicker to put on than a wrap sling and the central panel provides good support, and often they come with extra details such as pockets. Mei tais are good for slightly older babies and toddlers, particularly as back carriers, but many are not supportive enough for newborns.

Soft Structured Carriers

Soft structured carriers are the most similar to the popular baby carrier sold in specialty shops, with the important addition of providing good back support for both baby and wearer. They also give support out to the baby's knees by keeping their legs in a froggy position, rather than "crotch dangling," as is so common with modern commercial carriers. They are the most "manly" looking, usually due to the buckles and straps required to fit them, and are therefore popular with dads! While they can be used with smaller babies (usually with extra inserts) they are most suited to use with older babies and toddlers (particularly for back carries).

Babywearing Guidelines and Cautions

Many parents are tempted to wear their baby facing outwards in a sling or carrier, believing that the baby needs to be stimulated by the big wide world around them and would get bored facing constantly into the wearer's chest. In fact the very reverse is true—for babies facing outwards in a carrier, the world can become a scary, over-stimulating place very quickly: indeed, many babies, particularly younger ones, find it hard to switch off from all of the stimulation the world provides and may get very upset and find it difficult to fall to sleep facing outwards.

Physiologically speaking, carrying a baby facing outwards also curves their spine in a very unnatural way. If you remember that you need to hold a baby with a natural "C"-shaped curve to his spine, it becomes obvious that this is only achieved when the baby is carried facing inwards, allowing his body to mold around the carrier's body and the baby's spine to rest in a more natural curvature. By contrast, holding a baby facing outwards causes an artificial hollow in his back as he tries to brace himself and can also chafe his inner thighs (not to mention squashing a boy's delicate bits!).

Once your baby is a little older you might find carrying him on your back works better for you both, allowing your baby the comfort of being carried in an anatomically correct position while being able to look out on the world when he chooses and to rest his head on your back when he becomes tired and over-stimulated.

Babywearing International (see resources) advises parents to follow these guidelines when babywearing:

- Ensure the baby's back and torso are well supported: make sure the baby is not curled up such that his chin is pressed to his chest or his airway is otherwise compressed. Ensuring that you can put two fingers vertically between the baby's chin and chest is a good guide.

- Carry babies how they would be held in-arms: well-designed front baby carriers hold babies snugly against the chest and near the caregiver's face.
- Monitor the baby at all times. Make sure nothing obstructs the face or impedes breathing.
- Be aware of movements and surroundings. In general, don't do something while wearing a child that shouldn't be done while simply holding them. Avoid heat sources, bumping and jarring motions, and other hazardous situations.

An easy way to remember the safety guideline is by using the acronym TICKS (used by the British Association of Babywearing Instructors—www.babi.me.uk):

Tight
In view at all times
Close enough to kiss
Keep chin off chest
Supported back

The diagrams opposite and on page 40 show the basic technique for tying a wrap sling.

Babywearing is also a great way for dads to bond with babies and is even better when teamed with some movement such as dancing or a brisk walk. It is quite common for a baby to cry once placed in a sling. This does not mean that they hate the sling—it just means that you need to move, so get dancing.

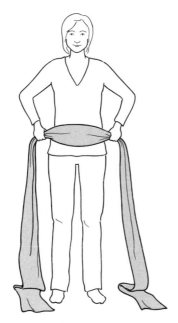

Find the middle of the wrap

Wrap it around your waist, cross it behind you and bring the straps up and over the back of your shoulders

Pass the straps through the band around your waist and cross them

Take the straps around your waist, cross them behind you and bring them back to the front

Tie in a double knot at the side.
If there isn't enough fabric to bring
it around to your front, just
tie it at your back

Fan all the fabric out over
your shoulders and place baby
in the sling as per the diagram
on page 34

Deep Bathing

The uterus is a wet, warm place. The world as we know it is dry and relatively cold, so imagine what a huge transition your baby has already made just by living in air! For some babies a nice deep, warm (around 98.6°F or 37°C) bath can stop their tears in seconds and one wonders if to them it feels like "going home."

For babies, it is a return to that warm and wet familiar environment they lived in for nine long months. French obstetrician Frederick Leboyer is a great advocate of the use of deep, warm water baths for newborn babies, and his groundbreaking book *Birth without Violence*, published in 1974, includes much information on their calming properties. Addressing the question of how to calm newly born babies, Leboyer says, "It is easy. The child is leaving the warmth and softness of its mother's stomach. We can ensure that it finds a similar warmth and softness elsewhere. We should not place a newborn baby on metal scales, so cold and hard. Nor in material that feels rough after the mother's smoothness and warmth. We should place it, in fact, replace it—in water!"

You can buy one of the new bucket-shaped baby bath tubs, which seem to offer a more natural experience than bathing a baby in a regular baby bath and certainly there will be the benefits of total body submersion. They also hold the baby in a more natural fetal position, which can make some babies feel more secure. My preference, however, is always for mom or dad to go into the big bath with the baby, as co-bathing provides the ultimate security and experience for your baby and is also really enjoyable for you. Deep bathing also gives lots of skin-to-skin contact, which in itself is a wonderful baby calmer, as these mothers found:

> I loved having my baby in the bath with me, and he adored it, floating around almost submersed in the warm water, then usually he fed and fell asleep on me, bliss.

> I loved being in the bath with him and having loads of skin to skin.

> We are family bath converts! We always bath our babies with one of us in with them, and the bath is so big we sometimes all squeeze in for a true family bath!

Feeding

If your baby is hungry nothing will placate him, so watch for your baby's early hunger cues, which are signs he may show before he cries for food. Remember that crying is always a *late* indicator that your baby is hungry.

As we have already seen in chapter 2, early hunger cues include:

- licking lips and opening and closing of the mouth
- sucking fists, lips, or tongue
- rooting
- fidgeting
- fussy behavior

It's worth bearing in mind that your baby may not always be hungry for a full feed; he may want a quick drink, a quick snack, or just some comfort sucking. Feeding on demand is vitally important with young babies and I have devoted a whole chapter to this later in the book (see chapter 9). We have already seen that, as well as providing important nutrition, babies also find sucking the ultimate relaxation and comfort tool, as well as helping the skull bones to return to their normal position after birth.

> I remember a huge surge of love (endorphins?) as I sat sleepily feeding my newborn in the quiet of the night . . . lovely!

> I looked forward to the end of every day with my baby, the time when I would allow myself to give him my total attention—feeding, bathing, holding him close to my skin. This is when we were both at our calmest and most happy.

Movement

If you think about life for a baby before they were born, the chances are you might imagine them swirling around inside their watery home. Just think about how much your baby moved around inside of you and all of the kicks that you felt when you were pregnant. For him, the weightlessness and water supporting his tiny body allowed him, to move in ways that he will not be able to recreate for many months now that he is "earth side." Think, too, about the movements you contributed to your baby. The pregnant uterus is a constantly moving space, for example Braxton Hicks contractions would squeeze your baby many times a day, particularly towards the end of your pregnancy, just like a reassuring, gentle massage, and each time you moved, your baby moved around inside of you too.

Now, think about how odd it must be for your baby to lie still for much of his time now that he is born; his own body unable to move in the same way he did in utero and your body around him not moving as it once did. Many babies love movement, whether that means being rocked to sleep in your arms, danced around to music by dad, or bounced on grandma's knee. Providing you support your baby's head and neck well, you will find he is quite robust and perhaps enjoys bigger movements than you may have been initially comfortable with. You could try dancing, swaying from side to side, going for a brisk walk, or anything where you really move.

The great side effect of this for you is that when you move around and exercise, your pituitary gland will secrete endorphins, those natural happiness hormones, which are great mood enhancers. Exercise also increases the release of serotonin and noradrenaline; low levels of both of these neurotransmitters have been linked to depression. Going for a brisk walk outside can be a life saver for many new moms.

At our BabyCalm™ classes we often encourage parents to dance with their babies, especially to some great upbeat music, and we tend to find dads are particularly good at doing the baby dance!

> My husband danced around with my son all evening every evening for weeks as it was the only way we could get him to stop crying.

Noise

The uterus is a really noisy place! Babies in utero are used to constant sound around them from the mother's circulatory system, especially her heartbeat, her digestive system, and the rush of blood through the umbilical cord. After being accustomed to all that noise imagine how unsettling it must have been for your baby to be born into a world of relative silence that's punctuated with unexpected, different noises. In utero the sound never changed from the same volume and the same tempo, but now your baby is here he is dealing with so many different sounds.

Many babies respond really well to being played womb-like sounds, or what is commonly known as "white noise." White noise is a combination of sound frequencies, including all of the tones that are audible to a human. It is estimated that white noise contains 20,000 different tones. This combination of sound frequencies is said to mimic the sound of the uterus and have a very calming effect, not just on babies, but adults too.

Many of the moms in my classes comment on how much white noise has helped them to calm their babies, often with surprising, but welcome side effects too:

White noise for my son was like flicking a switch. He used to grunt and writhe around a lot when he was tired, and he wasn't a baby who wanted to feed to sleep for some reason, so I would swaddle him and put my radio onto static . . . and later I bought a CD. The funniest thing was, we stayed at my mom's one weekend and my sister, who is a terrible insomniac, was also staying. She was staying in the room right next to us and she said it was the best night's sleep she'd ever had, because she could hear the radio through the wall. After that she downloaded a white noise app for her phone. Even at seventeen months, if my little one is having trouble settling off to sleep, I put the white noise CD on and he goes off so quickly. I was skeptical but it really does work. And it genuinely doesn't bother/disturb us as we worried it would.

We got a wave machine [a white noise device that makes nature sounds] as a gift before we even had kids. I recognized right away with baby number one that he seemed soothed by it. So I bought a "baby" version, which has been there every night for all three kids and has traveled all over the world with us. I wouldn't be without my white noise!

A study at Queen Charlotte's Hospital in London[19] found that 80 percent of newborn babies fell asleep within five minutes in response to white noise compared with only 25 percent who fell asleep within the five minutes without white noise.

You can replicate the sound of the uterus in many ways that don't have to cost much at all, including leaving your radio tuned to static, doing some vacuuming, or using a fan in the room your baby sleeps in. In fact, research in America[20] found that a ceiling fan operating in the room of a sleeping baby reduced SIDS risk by 72 percent. You can also buy specially produced white noise CDs cheaply, and the benefit of these is that they can be played on loop and the volume lowered as your baby settles. It is worth leaving the white noise playing while your baby sleeps, as well as just using it to settle him, as the noise can help your baby to settle again during the normal sleep cycles, when he might otherwise wake.

Pacifiers

Pacifier use is highly prevalent in the UK. The Avon Longitudinal Study found that nearly 60 percent of the 10,950 babies in the sample had used a pacifier by four weeks of age.[9] Pacifier use creates possibly the biggest division of opinions in the parenting world, with many in favor of their calming properties and others vehemently anti them. Interestingly, there are marked differences in pacifier use around the world: as we have seen, 60 percent of British babies in the Avon survey used pacifiers, while in the United Arab Emirates 99.1 percent used breastfeeding as a soothing method with less than 10 percent using pacifiers to soothe their babies.[10]

On the positive side, research has suggested that using pacifiers reduces the risk of cot death (SIDS—sudden infant death syndrome),[11,12] though nobody is quite sure why. This research has led to the American Academy of Pediatrics and the UK's Lullaby Trust recommending using a pacifier at every sleep to reduce the risk of SIDS, but waiting until one month in the case of introducing a pacifier to breastfed babies so that breastfeeding can become established. The research methodology though has been highly criticized and the results questioned.

Suckling is nature's best comforter, so if you are breastfeeding you already have all of the equipment you need, although many breastfeeding moms still choose to use pacifiers to help dads to calm their baby or for when they need time alone. You should be aware that pacifier use could affect the success of breastfeeding and may cause your baby to wean earlier than you would like. If you are formula feeding, however, you might find that you are helped greatly by the use of a pacifier, which gives your baby a chance to suck when not being fed.

Skull Compression during Birth and the Need to Suck

Another theory concerning the calming effect of pacifier use is related to the physiology of your baby's skull. During labor your baby's cranial bones moved and overlapped. They then usually return to their normal position over a few days after the birth, mostly via the process of your baby sucking, which causes movement of the upper and lower jaw to stimulate the base of your baby's skull via the palate. Sometimes, however, things don't return to normal and often abnormal skull compression becomes noticeable due to the baby's feeding habits and the need to suck much more than usual. If the baby's vagus nerve, the cranial nerve, which is directly linked to digestion, is compressed during pregnancy or birth this can also have a noticeable effect on a baby's digestive system, causing him pain. All of this is more likely to happen if your labor was long or your baby presented at a funny angle.

There is, however, no scientific evidence to support this, but anecdotally many chiropractors and cranial osteopaths agree that the calming effects of sucking can be seen. A recent literature review[13] reported: "Our findings reveal that chiropractic care is a viable alternative to the care of infantile colic and congruent with evidence-based practice, particularly when one considers that medical care options are no better than placebo or have associated adverse events."

What Is Chiropractic And Cranial Osteopathy?

Many parents swear by chiropractic and osteopathic treatment for their babies. Both are forms of alternative medicine that aim to restore the structure and function of the body to full health, largely by manually manipulating joints, muscles, and the skeletal system to restore proper alignment and function. The aim is to restore balance to the body and remove tension and pain. Treatment of young babies tends to focus on the skull and neck in the belief that a baby's head can be compressed and/or their neck and spine placed under stress during late pregnancy and the birth itself. I have heard many positive comments about both methods of treatment and indeed have used them for my own children with good outcomes. I often recommend treatment to new moms with fractious babies, particularly if their birth was long or resulted in an assisted delivery or intervention, i.e. forceps, ventouse, or Caesarean.

Possible Risks of Pacifier Use

The use of pacifiers is not without risk. Science suggests there is a definite link between pacifier use and pediatric ear infections. A Finnish study[14] found the occurrence of acute otitis media (ear infection) was 29 percent lower among children whose parents had been told to limit pacifier use. Dutch researchers[15] also found that pacifier use was a risk factor for ear infections.

Research also suggests that pacifiers can cause orthodontic changes with long-term (more than two years) use. Scandinavian researchers[16] found that there was a high prevalence of orthodontic problems (posterior crossbite) in pacifier users, but at least two years of pacifier use was necessary to produce a significant problem.

Lastly, one piece of recent research[17] found that there was a negative correlation between breastfeeding and use of a pacifier. However, another recent review of research[18] found that pacifier use in healthy term breastfeeding infants, started from birth or after breastfeeding is established, did not significantly affect the prevalence or duration of exclusive and partial breastfeeding up to four months of age.

Pacifier Use Guidelines

- Wait until breastfeeding is well established (FSID suggest breastfeeding moms don't use a pacifier for the first four weeks).
- Only give your baby a pacifier when they really need it (i.e., to calm crying or help a fractious baby sleep) but take the pacifier away when the baby is calm to prevent the pacifier use becoming habitual.
- Use pacifiers with a specially shaped orthodontic teat.
- Try to get rid of the pacifier by six months of age; by this time the benefits have pretty much served their purpose— longer use can take you more into the negative camp.
- Always be led by your baby. If your baby won't take a pacifier, don't persevere—listen to them!

Skin-to-Skin Contact

Skin-to-skin contact is so important, not only for calming your baby but also for helping him to thrive. It is a major element in bonding and why you were probably encouraged to hold your baby skin to skin right after his birth in order to encourage the release of oxytocin, the calming hormone of love and bonding.

> When we were trying to establish breastfeeding with our baby, I loved being in the bath with him and having loads of skin to skin; it really helped us to bond and calm him.

> Skin to skin after my second C-Section made a huge difference to bonding compared to my first baby. It was wonderful and felt completely right.

The benefits of this close contact do not end after the first couple of hours, but they can continue for a lifetime. If you think about it, although we handle our babies many, many times every day it's actually quite rare that we touch them skin to skin for very long. Very often when we hold them our babies are dressed or we are busy trying to dress them, taking a diaper off and putting another on, and so on. Making a special time each day to have uninterrupted skin-to-skin contact with your baby can work miracles, for him and for you. A great way to do this is through infant massage.

In her book, *Infant Massage: A Handbook for Loving Parents*, Vimala McClure says, "Infant massage can promote the kind of parenting that the attentive mother was able to provide. Its benefits go far beyond the immediate physiological gains. As you massage your baby regularly, you will discover that you develop a bond with your child that will last a lifetime."

Although there are many baby massage classes available, you don't need a special education in order to massage your baby: the important point is that you touch your baby calmly, respectfully, and lovingly. Massaging your baby can turn into a wonderfully special time to spend with your baby well beyond the first few weeks, as these moms found:

> It was natural to me. I had no other reason. I have always responded immediately and wholly to massage so I assumed my baby would too, so it was very instinctive for me to massage him.

> I had taught baby massage for six years before I had a baby, so being able to massage my own baby was like coming home. Blissful, tender, and warm. I loved it!

> I gave him his first massage at about three days old; it was the first time I had seen him naked. It was the most amazing moment. He is now 5 years old and still gets regular massages.

BabyCalm™ suggests a very simplified baby massage routine, which we call BabyCalm™ touch therapy. The most important aspect of this touch therapy is that it is simple and baby led; please do not worry about it being perfect, as these are only very rough suggestions to start you off so that you can discover your own way of touching your baby that works for both of you. Above all else enjoy this special time with your baby and remember that you do not need to be an expert.

BabyCalm™ Simple Eight-Step Baby Touch Therapy

Before you start, make sure the room is warm, remove any jewelry, and switch off the phone! Do not massage your baby right after a feed, and if your baby is not in the mood

or cries during the massage then stop and pick another
time when he is happier and calmer.

1. Calm yourself before you begin, take a few good, slow,
   deep breaths (try breathing in to a count of seven and
   out to eleven), relax your body, and then talk to your
   baby and ask their permission to touch them. This
   might seem slightly odd, but it opens channels of communication between you and your baby and also treats
   them with respect.
2. Remove all of their clothes and diaper and hold them
   close, feeling each part of their tiny body and getting to
   know them on an even deeper level. This is even more
   wonderful if you are skin to skin with your own top off!
   Sometimes you may not go past this step—do whatever feels right for you and your baby.
3. Pour a generous amount of edible, unscented massage oil, preferably organic and cold pressed for quality
   (e.g., organic sunflower) and rub it into your hands so
   they are nice and warm (never scrimp on oil). Stroke
   your baby gently from head to foot, talking or singing
   to them while you do. Don't worry if they don't main-
   tain eye contact; that's very common and it doesn't
   mean they are not enjoying it. Little babies may prefer
   to lie in their mom's or dad's lap or arms.
4. Now start to concentrate on the legs. Gently turn your
   hands and stroke outwards from the top of the thigh
   to the end of the toes with one hand after the other.
   After a few strokes you could take both hands to the
   top of the thigh and create a tube effect, squeezing
   all the way to the foot, and once you arrive at the foot
   squeeze and hold if your baby likes it. Repeat with the
   other leg.

5. Bring the legs gently up to the chest in a bicycling motion—ALWAYS letting the baby lead and then, with your baby leading, bring their legs up in a frog-type position and sway from side to side resting your palm on the baby's chest. (Avoid this if your baby has any hip issues.)

6. Moving onto the tummy, gently cup your right palm over your baby's belly, then using both hands in a wave-type motion move in a clockwise motion, up the ascending colon (or large intestine), across the transverse colon, and down the descending colon. Then use the side of your hand and move down in a wave-type motion (avoid this if your baby still has an umbilical hernia or cord stump).

7. Moving onto the chest, place both hands in the center of the chest and move outwards, gently "opening" the chest. Then, placing your right hand on their right shoulder, hug and glide down to their left hip. Repeat with your left hand. Note that little babies often do not like this, so be baby led.

8. Moving onto the arms, repeat as for legs. With your baby leading, bring both arms into the chest and clap, then open out to their sides. Make this a game and be baby led. Turn baby onto their tummy if you think they would like it (a towel rolled underneath their head and chest is often more comfortable for little babies—or, even better, do this with your baby on your lap) and bring your right hand to their left shoulder, hug and glide down to their bottom, repeat for your left hand/ their right shoulder. *Always end with lots of hugs and kisses!*

Swaddling

Swaddling is a centuries old, yet increasingly popular technique used to calm babies. Many people believe that swaddling can help a baby to feel as if he is still being held when you need to put him down and also helps to inhibit his startle (Moro) reflex, which many babies find upsetting. Also, you may find that your baby sleeps for longer when he is put down swaddled and calms quicker if he is upset. However, many people are very against swaddling, saying it can cause numerous problems, as well as not being very respectful to the baby.

You need to bear in mind that swaddling is intended to be used as a substitute for physical contact with you, so if you are holding, babywearing, or sleeping with your baby they do not need to be swaddled as well, as they have the real thing and nothing can replace you!

If you are feeding on demand it's very important that you don't miss your baby's early hunger signals as they may be less obvious when your baby is swaddled. I tend to find therefore that swaddling is often better suited to babies who are formula fed rather than breastfed. Lastly, remember that swaddled babies still need lots of physical skin-to-skin contact and hugs.

If you would like to swaddle your baby it's worth noting that FSID (Foundation for the Study of Infant Deaths) recommends swaddling with caution, following the guidelines below:

- Never swaddle over your baby's head or near his face.
- Never swaddle your baby if he is ill or has a fever.
- Make sure your baby does not overheat and only swaddle with a breathable/thin fabric.
- Only swaddle your baby until he can roll over.*
- *Always* place your baby to sleep on his back.
- Do not swaddle tightly across your baby's chest.

- Do not swaddle tightly around your baby's hips and legs. His legs should be free to "froggy up" into a typical newborn position.
- Lastly, start to swaddle as soon as possible; do not swaddle a three-month-old baby if he has not been swaddled before.

*The American Academy of Pediatrics recommends swaddling for babies 0 to 14 weeks.

For guidance on how to swaddle your baby see the diagrams on pages 55-56.

BabyCalm™ Easy 5-Step Swaddling Technique

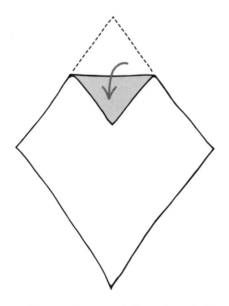

Fold over the top of the BabyCalm™ swaddle sheet to make a triangle.

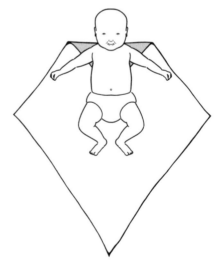

Place your baby with the top of the fold level with his neck.

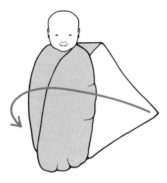

Now, bring the last remaining flap of material to your left and wrap it, all the way around your baby, using his own weight to keep the wrap secure.

Ensure the fabric is wrapped loosely over the baby's chest and hips – you are looking for tightness over the arms and tummy only.

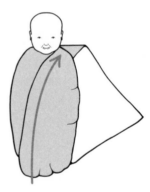

Tuck your baby's right arm at his side, take hold of the top left-hand corner and bring it down and over your baby. Tuck the sheet under his left-hand side.

Bring the bottom of the sheet up to the baby's left-hand shoulder, hold the baby's arm to his side and tuck the fabric underneath his arm, torso and bottom.

Taking Your Baby Outside

Many babies stop crying the minute they hit the open air. I'm not sure if this is because they are usually moving about, such as being pushed over cobbles in a stroller, bouncing in a sling, or traveling along in a car, or just because of the change in air, but it can often have quite a dramatic effect.

Also it can work wonders for you to get outside and go for a head-clearing walk if you have been inside with a crying baby for quite some time. Many moms have told me that they really value their walks with their babies as not only does it get them out and about and help to release endorphins through the exercise, but it is also a good way for them to get to meet other new moms and have a chat. Some moms I have worked with mention that this may be the only time they speak to another adult all day and is therefore vital for their sanity.

Going outside was a literal breath of fresh air! I calmed down, baby calmed down, and I somehow seemed to get back in touch with the world.

I knew that going out would make me feel better, but some days I just couldn't bring myself to do it. Because there was nowhere to go or no one to see it kind of seemed pointless, but cabin fever was worse. So even a trip to the store meant fresh air, and the times I did it, it made me feel better.

Tiger-in-the-Tree Hold

Very often when we try to calm a baby we do so by holding them facing to us, often cradling their faces and looking into their eyes, yet for an over-stimulated baby, facing them away from us (and that stimulation) for a short while can often work so much better. One tip I learned from a baby yoga class was a position known as "tiger in the tree," holding a baby facing away from you and downwards with their head firmly supported in the crook of your elbow and holding their crotch with the same hand. Don't forget that your baby is used to being upside down and on his side in utero so you may find that this "tiger-in-the-tree" position is magical and will stop your crying baby in an instant! Try this pose for a brief period, indoors, specifically for calming your baby.

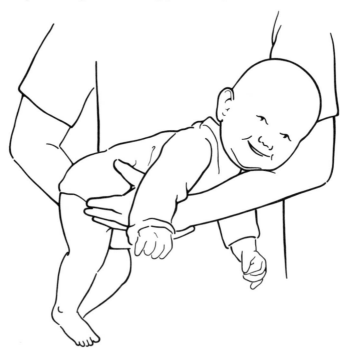

It works even better when you dance while holding your baby in this position. I vividly remember in the yoga class how silent the room grew once we danced holding our babies like sleepy tigers dangling from a tree branch, and however loud their cries were at the start of the dance you could hear a pin drop by the end.

> The tiger-in-the-tree hold was the biggest revelation to me and my husband; what an amazing little secret! Not only did it instantly settle our baby, whereby you could hold her close and calm her, but also wander around and have a hand free. Fantastic!

> Our daughter loved the tiger-in-the-tree hold and it really seemed to help settle her. I think it had a lasting effect, though, as to this day (at the age of nearly six) she still loves being a stripy tiger with orange and black stripes and running all over the house!

Note: Please remember that a baby should always be placed on his back to sleep.

Chapter 4

Parenting around the World

If someone told you they knew a secret to help your baby sleep better, cry less, and learn better, you would certainly be interested.

—**Dr. Maria Blois, author of *Babywearing***

Have you seen pictures of mothers in rural Africa with their babies held securely on their backs with brightly colored fabrics? Mexican babies bound to their mothers with rainbow-striped rebozos? Photographs of mothers in Asia, working in fields with their infants tied securely to them in a mei tai carrier? Or images of Inuit babies snuggled in warm fleece-lined papooses?

It amazes me that people think babywearing is a new and modern phenomenon when actually it is as old as time. I was stopped in the street many times while "wearing" one of my children in a sling. Older people and even health visitors said things like, "Oh, we didn't have those new-fangled, trendy things in my day—a stroller was good enough for us." In fact, it is our strollers, pushchairs, and travel systems that are "new-fangled"!

Babywearing and baby carrying is not new, it is not trendy, it is not a passing phase, and it was not invented by a particular parenting school or brand. Rather it is normal and natural and to many parents around the world it is a practical necessity.

Babywearing takes us back to our hunter–gatherer ancestry. As I have already mentioned in chapter 3, the menfolk would go out and hunt for meat, while the women would gather fruit, vegetables, firewood, and more, all the while with their young carried on their backs. They had no choice other than to take their babies with them! In her book *Population Pressure and Cultural Adjustment*, Virginia Abernethy describes the babywearing practices of the !Kung tribe, a hunter–gatherer tribe who lived in Southern Africa: "The !Kung Bushmen have been called 'affluent,' but a mother carries her child with her at all times up to four years of age; this is equivalent to about 4,900 miles in the course of gathering the plant foods which are the Bushmen's primary subsistence resource. On each trek a woman carries the child both ways, and on the return trip is also loaded with several days' supply of roots, nuts, berries, and firewood."

Tribal Parenting

I have already mentioned that one of the most mind-opening books I have read since having children is *The Continuum Concept* by Jean Liedloff. In the 1970s, Jean spent two and a half years in the South American jungle with the indigenous Indians, the Yequana tribe, and was astounded at how differently they raised their young in comparison to Western culture. Jean frequently observed how calm and happy the young Yequana members were, compared to Western infants. One particular point that she noted was the amount of "in arms" time the infants had.

> Babes in arms almost never cried and, fascinatingly, did not wave their arms, kick, arch their backs, or flex their hands and feet. They sat quietly in their slings or slept on someone's hip—exploding the myth that babies need

to flex to "exercise." They also did not throw up unless extremely ill and did not suffer from colic. When startled during the first months of crawling and walking, they did not expect anyone to go to them but rather went on their own to their mother or other caretakers for the measure of reassurance needed before resuming their explorations. Without supervision, even the smallest tots rarely hurt themselves. Is their "human nature" different from ours? Some people actually imagine that it is, but there is, of course, only one human species. What can *we* learn from the Yequana tribe?

In his book *Childhood: A Multicultural View*, Melvin Konner also discusses the similarities of tribal parenting with other primates and the stark differences with Western culture:

For instance in hunting and gathering societies like the Baka and the !Kung, infants are carried by the mother most of the time and are nursed several times an hour. . . . All these seemingly strange things are also true of our closest monkey and ape relatives. During our evolution, the constant closeness served several functions: mothers stood between babies and creatures that might eat them; they kept the babies warm with the warmth of their own bodies. . . . Do these evolutionary facts mean we must keep mothers and babies in constant contact? Certainly not. . . . Nevertheless it is not surprising that some mothers and infants in our society find themselves drifting back toward an ancient evolutionary pattern.

I should say here that I first bought this book as an undergraduate on the advice of my developmental psychology lecturer, Dr. James Demetre. I have to confess I didn't read it for another fifteen years until I had my own children and my curiosity was piqued. There is something about having your own children that opens doorways in your mind to a new, deeper understanding, interest, and empathy for both parents and babies that can never exist as a non-parent. It has now become one of my favorite books and I frequently dip in and out, hoping to absorb some of its wisdom. (And if Dr. Demetre ever reads this: thank you so much for the recommendation. I'm only sorry it took me so long to respond to it!)

What Can We in the West Learn from Tribal Parenting?

It is clear that babywearing was born out of necessity thousands of years before Dr. William Sears coined the phrase in the 1980s, though he did much to spearhead a Western resurgence. Babywearing enables mothers around the world to return to their chores, continue their daily routine, and provide food for their families. It is we, in the West, who are the odd ones out, who put our babies down at every available opportunity, and invent more and more new gadgets to replace our arms, our heartbeats, our warmth, and our movement. The minute our babies are born we start putting them down alone and we may wonder why they protest. Think what would happen if we embraced the babywearing normality of our hunter–gatherer roots. Would we see a change in our baby's behavior? Would that change reflect into toddlerdom and beyond?

Scientific research agrees strongly here too. It seems that not only does babywearing result in significantly reduced crying,[21] it also promotes the bond between parent and child.[22] As Dr. Sears says (on askdrsears.com), "Babywearing means changing your mindset of what babies are really like. New parents often envision babies as lying quietly in a crib, gazing passively at dangling mobiles and picked up and carried only to be fed and played with and then put down. You may think that 'up' periods are just dutiful intervals to quiet your baby long enough to put him down again. Babywearing reverses this view. Carry your baby in a sling many hours a day, and then put her down for sleep times and tend to your personal needs."

How Other Mammals Carry Their Young

We can find many other examples of mothers carrying their babies of course. When you look at other species you realize quite how normal it is for mammalian mothers to carry their young. Here again we are the odd ones out—we are the only species on this planet that puts our babies into wheeled contraptions and pushes them around! Perhaps it is time we learned a lesson from our mammalian counterparts? After all they don't seem to suffer from the extreme fatigue, persistent crying, colic, and feeding problems as human babies do. Could it be that one of the biggest differences comes from mammalian babies being "in arms," while our Western human babies lie in their strollers?

This point really hit home when I was visiting a zoo one spring with my then three-year-old daughter. Standing at the monkey enclosure I saw that the spring baby boom had arrived at the zoo and everywhere were cute little baby monkeys, holding onto their mothers tightly, suckling as their mothers swung from one branch to the next. As I turned away from the monkey enclosure I saw a sea of Maclarens, Quinnys, Bugaboos, and the like, all the colors of the rainbow, wheels and handles everywhere. Babies and toddlers sat facing away from their moms, clutching pacifiers and soft toys. Some of the babies were crying and the moms were jiggling the strollers from side to side or pushing them to and fro to calm them back to sleep.

I couldn't help but stare at the sea of strollers and human moms frantically trying to calm their wailing babies and then looking back to the monkey moms, all in physical contact with their calm babies, as they looked back at me with matched curiosity . . . and I felt a stab of sadness for that innate knowledge and connection we have lost.

THE IMPORTANCE OF TUMMY TIME

I feel that one of the biggest indicators that our babies do not spend enough time in our arms and too much time on their backs is the growing problem of positional plagiocephaly or "flat head syndrome." Positional plagiocephaly usually occurs when a baby spends too long lying on his back and exerts pressure on the back of his skull, causing flattening at the back of the head. Special helmets can be purchased to fix the problem, but the answer is so much simpler— remove the cause and you remove the problem. It seems that nature is telling us that babies are not meant to spend so much time lying on their backs.

As diagnostic criteria are not yet fully defined it is hard to estimate the incidence of positional plagiocephaly: at the strictest definition it is estimated to affect 1 in 300 infants, while at the other end of the spectrum estimates rise to an incidence in 48 percent of babies under the age of one.[23] Parents are frequently advised that while babies should always be placed on their backs to sleep, they should spend some time each day in "tummy time."[24] Many parents don't realize that babywearing, with the baby facing inwards naturally, as they should always be, is very similar to tummy time and carries all the same benefits, so if your baby doesn't like being placed on his tummy you may be relieved to know that babywearing is just as beneficial, but often much more enjoyable for the baby and for you!

The Benefits of Babywearing for Parents

We know that babywearing has deep roots in our evolutionary history and has many more benefits than being a handy way to transport your baby when out and about. For example, I always remind parents that slings can be worn indoors too (they are especially useful in the early days), where they can be wonderful calming tools, great developmental aids, and, perhaps most importantly of all, give you two hands back!

One of the least well known benefits of babywearing, however, is the calming effect it has on the parent. Research has shown that when mothers are in frequent close proximity with their babies their anxiety and stress levels are reduced.[25] Given all of this ancient knowledge, modern scientific wisdom, and maternal intuition, it is hard to understand why babywearing isn't more popular. One has to ask why so many of today's parenting experts advocate putting the baby down alone as much as possible and why so many moms are worried about "making a rod for their back" by holding their babies too much. How did logic, evidence, reason, and wisdom get so sidetracked by well-marketed, slickly packaged, poorly researched parenting advice?

One person I haven't yet mentioned in relation to babywearing is the father. Babywearing is great for dads, as a wonderful way of being close to and forging a bond with their new baby, particularly where the mom is breastfeeding (and the dad instantly has a calming disadvantage due to his obvious lack of breasts!), as it provides a great tool for him to calm his baby.

One other point you may not wish to share with your male partner is that it also draws a lot of female attention! Men never look as cute as when they are carrying a small baby in a sling and women can't help but look admiringly. My husband often comments that, had he known of the female-charming properties of babywearing while he was single, he would have borrowed a baby for the day to attract female attention!

Dads tend to prefer more "manly" carriers (usually in black, and preferably with buckles) and there are plenty of soft structured carriers that are anatomically good for baby and wearer that have the right look.

I'll finish this chapter with Sam's story of babywearing and how it has helped him as a father:

Sam's Story

When our son was born my wife wanted to buy a wrap sling, something soft and gentle to carry him in. I used to watch them going about their business in perfect harmony together; it was like an extension of the womb. However, I thought it looked complicated and I feared squashing my son so I didn't use it. I was waiting to buy a more structured and front-facing sling so my son could watch the world and be stimulated and we could go for walks. But when it came to trying more structured slings at three months, it somehow felt wrong to face him out so early and have his body supported by his crotch . . . and, speaking as a man, to be honest it looked painful!

I tried many different slings and in the end realized that they were not at all complicated to put on, however confusing and scary they looked . . . in fact I was even quite good at it! I learned how to carry my son anatomically correctly and for the first time I understood the benefits of babywearing. . . . It wasn't just for my wife . . . my son loved being worn by me too . . . it felt amazing.

I started to view the use of slings very differently; they were not just a form of travel or a means to free up one's hands, but a way of being closer to one's baby . . . in kissing distance! I loved being able to stroke his head, his back, and his bum. I didn't want him facing the world, but rather nestled safely into me. Joking aside . . . one of the merits was that I was able to watch all the films I had been "meaning to see." My wife would go to bed exhausted and I would pop my son into a sling and dance and sway while catching up on films. He would sleep soundly! There was no pounding the floor boards at night in our house!

I still babywear him today at almost two years of age and so does my wife, although not as much and for different reasons. Recently I was at home looking after him and my wife was out; it was the middle of the summer, he was hot, irritated, teething, and nothing would soothe him. So I popped him into a soft structured carrier on my front and took him for a walk as I stroked his bare legs and feet and kissed his forehead . . . he was soon relaxed, soothed, and fell asleep. I couldn't have imagined achieving that by any other means on my own that day . . . when I got home he stayed asleep in the sling as I swayed, watching a film.

Chapter 5

Understanding Normal Baby Sleep

People who say they sleep like a baby usually don't have one.
—Father Leo J. Burke

Society seems to judge much of your success and worth as a new mother by how much and for how long your baby sleeps, particularly at night. "Is he sleeping through yet?"; "Is he a good boy?"; "Does he let you sleep much?" were all frequent questions I was asked as a first-time mother, questions that made me feel anxious about my child's sleep and my abilities (or inabilities) to help him not wake in the night. That was with baby number one, but by babies two and three I just used to silently "grrrrr" to myself while nodding and giving a weak, sleep-deprived smile, and by baby number four woe-betide anybody who innocently asked me those questions as they would find themselves on the receiving end of a tyranny of rants and swear words!

I love my sleep and I pretty much slept away most of my teenage years and early twenties . . . and then it hit me, I gave birth to my first baby and my sleep has never been the same since. Oh yes, sleep is an elusive friend to me now, but I have something so much more wonderful in its place and if I didn't want my life to change I wouldn't have had children in the first place. That, in short, was the answer I ended up giving to anybody who asked me whether my babies were "good" or "sleeping through yet."

What Is a "Good Baby" Anyway?

I really don't understand why society thinks that a sleeping baby is a "good baby." By labeling some babies as "good," surely that implies the reverse is true and thus those who are not "sleeping through" will be labeled as "bad"? It seems that many of us have no understanding of the physiology of normal infant sleep. If we did there would certainly be no role for the myriad of "baby sleep trainers" out there, nobody would enquire about your baby's sleep, and no new mothers would be left feeling that they were failing in their role or wondering what was wrong with their babies because they don't sleep all night.

When a baby is in utero he borrows the circadian rhythms (or "body clock") of his mother as the sleepy hormone melatonin is passed to him via the placenta. Once a baby is born, however, this exchange of melatonin obviously ceases and it takes a baby's body a while to be able to regulate his rhythms as his mother's did for him. In fact it takes until at least two months[26] to get anywhere close and even longer, until around the age of four years, for his hormones to produce the same effects as an adult.

Biologically speaking, a young baby, particularly one under four months of age, really does not know the difference between night and day. We may feel sleepy when the sun sets, but for your little one, sundown is no different than sunrise. Some baby experts advocate teaching a baby the difference between night and day as early as possible, oftentimes from birth, by advocating black-out curtains, total quiet, avoiding eye contact, and other sensory stimulation, claiming that this will teach a baby to sleep through the night at a young age. In reality this cannot be the case: yes, the baby does become conditioned to communicate less at night, but at best this is because he has been trained not to do so, rather than understanding that it is night-time and therefore he must be tired and should sleep. What you may well end up with, if you follow this path, is a baby who will find it incredibly hard to sleep unless he has complete silence and a black-out curtain, which makes for very miserable experiences when on vacation or going out for the evening. When I had my firstborn many other new mothers marveled at my son's ability to "sleep anywhere," as he could sleep in bright daylight, in almost any position, and with almost any noise levels, including sleeping throughout a loud wedding disco at the age of two months. Did he possess some miraculous sleeping skill or was this ability normal for a baby who hadn't been taught to sleep with as little sensory stimulation as possible?

Forming Realistic Expectations of Your Baby's Sleep

As well as lacking the hormonal sleep regulators of an adult, a baby's sleep cycle is also hugely different from that of an adult. Small babies' sleep cycles are very simplistic and composed of two basic states, being quiet sleep (deep sleep) and active sleep (more alert sleep), and furthermore, each sleep cycle is about half the length (at around 45 minutes) of an adult sleep state (which lasts for around 90 minutes).

The differences between adults' and babies' sleep patterns made perfect biological sense in the days when our young needed to be alert to threats from predators, but their evolution has not yet caught up with the relative safety of the nursery. This is why a baby goes through a sleep cycle twice as quickly as an adult, and it is not hard to work out that they are likely to wake around twice as much as adults during the night; in fact they move into a light sleep state around once every 20 to 45 minutes. Once in that lighter sleep state babies are naturally more easy to wake should something alarm them, whatever that something may be. Why do babies wake so frequently though? What is alarming and arousing them? It is quite possible that on several occasions you'll have no idea why your baby is crying in the middle of the night when other times it may be plainly obvious to you.

Think about why you wake at night. For me, last night it was because I woke up cold to find the duvet had slipped off, because my husband was snoring, and because my four year old ran in at 6 AM and jumped on my bed. Sometimes I wake because I need to go to the toilet, sometimes I'm too hot, sometimes I'm scared of strange noises, sometimes I have disturbing dreams, sometimes I wake because my throat is dry and I need a drink. Sometimes I have no idea at all why I have awoken.

I wonder why we presume babies "should be able to sleep through by twelve weeks"? We should know that even if a baby does not cry out during the night, it is highly unlikely that they have slept through; indeed, it is highly likely that they will have woken, often several times, but they just didn't alert anyone to the fact. Just as I awoke for numerous reasons last night and you probably awoke for numerous different reasons, so babies wake for lots of reasons too.

So, is a baby really "good" or "contented" if they don't call out to us? Are we really "good parents" because our babies lie there, alone and awake, and don't need us? Dr. William Sears coined the phrase "shutdown syndrome" to describe what may potentially be happening in this scenario, which he described on his website AskDrSears.com: "Babies who are 'trained' not to express their needs may appear to be docile, compliant, or 'good' babies. Yet these babies could be depressed babies who are shutting down the expression of their needs, and they may become children who don't ever speak up to get their needs met and eventually become the highest-need adults."

What about the fact, too, that young babies need to feed frequently throughout the day and night? There is scientific research[27] that shows that having the expectation or desire for your baby to sleep through the night at an early age can conflict with a baby's need for frequent feeding. Here again, so many baby experts seem to believe that babies should function like adults, even suggesting "tanking up" during the day with milk, dream feeding (a late feed without arousing the baby), or moving onto "hungry baby" formula so that they have no need to wake for a feed during the night. These assumptions may be true for us, as grown adults, with our large stomachs and solid food intake, but for a small baby with a tiny tummy on a quickly digestible liquid diet it is just not realistic.

But What about the Angel Babies?

Of course there are some babies who require very little input from us at night, who fall asleep by themselves, and sleep for long stretches at night naturally. These "angel babies," as Tracy Hogg, author of *The Baby Whisperer*, refers to them, are just born that way. In this chapter I am not referring to the babies who sleep for long stretches naturally, for they are in a very small minority, rather I am referring to the majority of babies who wake and cry regularly.

Flynn, my second-born son, slept from 8 PM to 6 AM pretty much every night from about eight weeks of age, entirely of his own doing, and never wanted me in the night. Ironically, something that would make many new parents jump with joy left me feeling a little sad, as I enjoyed our snuggly night feeds, sitting there babe in arms thinking of all the other mothers doing the same thing at the same time. All babies are different and some babies are just like Flynn, natural-born sleepers, but I cannot stress enough that they are in the minority.

The most important point I would like to make in this chapter is that it is totally normal and healthy for young babies to wake frequently at night. If they wake frequently it is not a reflection on your parenting skills or a problem needing to be solved, unless you—and only you—feel it is a problem.

The Cruel Myth of "Sleeping Through" the Night

Scientists agree that regular night waking in young babies is both normal and common. One study[28] has found that at three months of age 46 percent of babies woke regularly at night, at six months of age 39 percent woke regularly, at nine months sleep appears to regress with 58 percent waking regularly, tailing off to 55 percent still waking regularly at night at twelve months. In the Avon Longitudinal Study[29] a sample of 640 infants showed that only 16 percent "slept through" at six months of age. Also, studies of parents' feelings about their baby's sleep[30] indicate that "nearly a third of all parents have significant problems with their child's sleep behavior."

I believe that it is about time society formed realistic expectations of a baby's sleeping habits. We must stop labeling the small minority of babies who do sleep through at a young age as "good" and we must stop judging parenting skills according to the quality of a baby's sleep!

In my work with new parents I find that helping them to have more realistic expectations of their baby's sleep patterns is key. Rather than trying to solve what they perceive as a problem of broken sleep, we should be helping them to be as relaxed and supported as possible during this normal period for all babies.

The focus should be on helping parents to cope, whether through longer paternity leave, better maternity pay, better funding for SureStart, HomeStart, and other similar family organizations, and better antenatal parenting preparation. I am not suggesting that just because frequent night waking is both normal and healthy for young babies, parents should feel guilty for sometimes feeling resentful of the tiny bundle depriving us of our sleep, because that would be impossible. Neither am I suggesting that you should just "grin and bear it" and wait for the blessed day when you look at your clock with disbelief at 7 AM and realize you have had a full eight hours' sleep. Sleepless nights with a small baby are really hard. You reach a new level of exhaustion that you can't appreciate until you have been there yourself, something these mothers discovered very quickly after their babies were born:

> No matter what someone tells you about sleep deprivation, I don't think you can ever fully understand it until you actually have your baby and experience it. I expected to feel tired with a newborn, but those first few months are beyond description. The reality of needing to be available twenty-four seven for feeding, diapers, cuddles, etc., and often having to do all those things back to back and then start the process all over again, was just so demanding physically and emotionally. But then surprisingly I found my body adapted and it didn't feel so onerous anymore and I came to really treasure those peaceful and intimate night feeds.

> I can't really remember that much about it in some ways. I know that it was tough going at the time, but we got through it. Sometimes I think it's really important for parents to hear that it's OK to be exhausted and feel like your brain has fallen out of your ears, because this too will pass.

> I can see why sleep deprivation is used as a form of torture; I was not prepared at all for the two- or three-hourly wake ups, but you just get through it and then it gets easier.

> Tiredness doesn't even begin to cover it. . . . I was a midwife but still felt totally overwhelmed by the reality of it.

I was totally exhausted, up and down, feeding/changing/ putting back down again, and then up again half an hour later. I felt guilty for poking my partner to wake up and help as I knew he had to be up for work.

When people used the quote "sleeping like a baby" I always thought that meant soundly and for at least seven hours, but I was awake all hours and it really took it out of me. I wish someone would have told me how hard it really was; mind you it's worth it for the rewards you get in the end.

Over the next two chapters we will look at some parent- and baby-friendly techniques you can use to help your baby to sleep for a little bit longer and settle back into a new sleep cycle without you having to get up four times in the night, but before that read Katie's story:

Katie's Story

Before I had a baby people kept asking me if we had got the nursery ready. They thought it a bit shocking that I hadn't bought the crib and decorated the room months in advance of my due date. I knew my baby would be sleeping in our room (in a Moses basket at first) for around six months as this was the advice we were given.

Many people have a mental image of a tiny baby tucked up in his own bed in his own room. My in-laws told me the story of how, when my husband was brought home from the hospital aged ten days, he was put upstairs to bed while they went out in the garden to drink champagne!

I knew that newborns woke in the night but I thought they woke every three hours. This terrified me and I thought I would never cope on so little sleep! How wrong I was . . .

I wasn't prepared for my first night in the hospital with Zachary as he wouldn't go to sleep in his plastic crib at all. Other babies on the ward were screaming and I was hot and exhausted and just wanted him to sleep. The midwife on duty showed me how to swaddle him, which helped, but the only thing that really got him to sleep was to cuddle him in bed with me. Then he slept a bit. I didn't sleep though as I was nervous anyway and worried a midwife would find us and tell me off.

At home he would wake every hour-and-a-half and want feeding. I had him in a Moses basket beside the bed, but even this arrangement felt inconvenient, as I had to sit up to check on him or lift him up. We swaddled him a bit, but there was a heat wave at that time and we were terrified of him overheating, so we kept unwrapping him! Of course, none of us were getting much sleep. I couldn't understand why he woke so often or how he could still be hungry all night, as he was getting plenty of milk in the day.

After a couple of weeks we took the side off the crib and wedged it against our bed, so Zachary slept on his own mattress, but right next to me where I could see him. It didn't particularly help his sleeping, as what he really wanted was to be actually in bed with me against my body. But I was frightened to do this as most of what I had heard about sleeping like this was negative. I was worried about the SIDS risk from him overheating, and I was also worried that we would never be able to get him out of our bed as he got older. I don't recall hearing or reading anything in favor of bed sharing that didn't mention an increased risk of SIDS. It seemed to be the case that, yes, your baby might sleep better, but they are more likely to die. Anyone who co-slept was a bit radical. It seems to be thought of as a bit odd to want your baby close to you at night as this is a private time for you and your partner. I never wanted my newborn baby out of my sight but we are supposed to deny our instincts at night-time.

I knew a couple of babies who had been in Special Care for a couple of weeks. They came out of hospital "perfect" sleepers and were put in their own rooms from day one. They slept for twelve hours anyway, so it didn't matter where they slept. I envied their good nights' sleep. Zachary continued to sleep like a newborn, waking every couple of hours, for weeks and weeks. Reading about it and listening to health visitors made me think this was a bit unusual, as he should be sleeping for at least four hours in one go at twelve weeks. What on earth was I doing wrong? I also read about the dreaded four-month sleep regression—not for us as there was nothing for him to regress to! I got good at just about coping with the sleep deprivation.

When you have a baby people are always asking you if he is a "good" baby, which basically means, does he sleep? It became almost a badge of honor to describe in great detail just how little sleep I was getting. What was most irritating about other people's reactions was the way they would say they would never be able to cope without a good night's sleep, so it was lucky their baby was such a good sleeper, managing to imply that both Zachary and I were freaks because he didn't sleep well. It is swings and roundabouts though as their good sleepers tended to be awake all day, whereas Zachary was a wonderful napper.

I heard about the local Children's Center's "Sleep Clinic," which got my hopes up for a solution until I discovered they teach controlled crying. This was not an option for me. To their credit, they do tell you not to do controlled crying until after six months. (Because babies don't need to wake in the night for food after the age of six months.)

I think my expectations of newborn sleep were reasonable, if optimistic, but what I didn't anticipate was how long the broken sleeping would continue. I thought after a few weeks he might only wake once a night. I was very tempted by controlled crying, and we did half-heartedly try it a couple of times out of sheer desperation. However, I had read about attachment parenting by this point and believed controlled crying was wrong. The only thing that worked for us was time. Eventually Zachary did occasionally sleep through—the first night he did was the day he learned to walk just before he turned ten months.

Chapter 6

Sleep Training Techniques

Whenever I held my newborn baby in my arms, I used to think that what I said and did to him could have an influence not only on him but on all whom he met, not only for a day or a month or a year, but for all eternity—a very challenging and exciting thought for a mother.

—Rose Kennedy, mother of US President J. F. Kennedy

As we learned in the last chapter, night waking is very common among young babies for a variety of good reasons. Newborns lack the hormonal regulators of sleep that adults possess and they have no concept of night and day. Add to this the much shorter sleep cycles that young babies experience, and the physiological need for them to feed around the clock, particularly if breastfeeding, and it becomes clear that their nocturnal behavior is totally normal. When you consider that estimates indicate approximately 25 percent of babies suffer from prolonged periods of excessive crying and that research shows us nearly 60 percent of babies still wake regularly at night at nine months of age,[31] it comes as no surprise that so many sleep-deprived parents seek ways to help with their baby's nocturnal sleep. Throw into the mix a consideration of the impact of lack of sleep and exhaustion upon a mother's emotional wellbeing, which in turn can have a knock-on effect on her bonding with her baby, and you can see why many individuals around the world make their livings as "baby sleep trainers."

Controlled Crying

For most of these desperate parents, help with their baby's sleeping will come in the form of sleep training involving managed crying episodes. Over the years encouraging a baby to sleep by leaving them to cry has been a mainstay of baby sleep advice, and many books come out recycling the same theories time and time again. The theories remain the same, although the names change, ranging from "controlled crying" to "graduated extinction," "cry it out," "wind down crying," "crying down," "pick up, put down," and "spaced soothing." For the rest of this chapter I will use the term "controlled crying," as it is the most familiar, but it applies to all the other theories as they are one and the same.

These methods usually also involve some environmental manipulation, such as the use of black-out curtains in the nursery and often use heavily structured routines in the day and a recommendation never to let your baby fall asleep in your arms, on the breast, or in the parental bed. Many psychologists, however, believe these methods are only a temporary fix and they can cause much more harm than good. As psychologist Oliver James says in his book *How Not to F Them Up*: "There is a great deal of evidence that very strict routines do not lead to so-called contented babies. . . . There is also good evidence that strict sleep routines do lead to more insecure, and to more irritable and fussy babies."

How Controlled Crying Makes Parents Feel

Even more worrying than the scientific evidence and mental health professionals' reservations is the fact that parents themselves often feel uncomfortable with this type of sleep training. I have met many, many mothers who have, at their wits' end and out of sheer desperation, resorted to using controlled crying, and I can willingly confess to being one of these myself with my firstborn. I have yet to meet any parents who have felt comfortable with the whole process; relieved that their babies are now sleeping through, yes most definitely, but happy with how they got there? Hardly ever. Here are just some of the comments I have heard on the subject of controlled crying:

> I was desperate, but it was awful, he cried so much. I cried too and just wanted to pick him up and end it.

> Oh, it definitely worked, she sleeps for twelve hours at night now, but I felt so guilty when we did the controlled crying, I've never seen her so upset before.

> We did try it, but only for two lots of two minutes. It felt like the longest two minutes of my life and I remember watching the seconds and the clock. I said to my husband, "I can't do this, it just isn't right," and he said, "No, it's horrible. I can't see how people can do it for longer periods." Something that a breastfeeding counselor said to me has always stuck in my mind, "If a friend was upset and crying, would you wait for five minutes before you comforted her?" I've not looked back since!

> With my second son I did try to sleep train him after taking tons of advice from well-meaning people as he was SO demanding and stroppy. But it broke me in half; I felt like someone was ripping my heart out and the guilt. . . . I still carry it now, years later.

> I remember crying because I was listening to my baby crying and not responding; it did make me feel slightly crazy. Again, just knowing now that it is because I was going against my instinct makes so much sense.

> I sat outside the bedroom door and wept like a crazy woman . . . but now I know I was just going against my instinct, so not crazy at all.

I had to stay downstairs with the baby monitor off while my husband stood outside the nursery door. I would have caved in and cuddled her; I'm not strong enough to hear her cry like that.

He got so upset he was sick all over himself. It was heartbreaking.

Now ask yourself this, what were these mothers' instincts telling them? It is so sad that the mothers to whom I spoke had to ignore their strong maternal instincts but felt they had no other choice. Some mothers, like this one, felt strong enough to listen to their instincts and ignore the sleep training advice constantly on offer to them:

Before having my baby, I had read a little bit about controlled crying and it just didn't seem to make sense to me, but as with everything else I thought, OK, let's wait and see. But when my baby cried, the internal pull to pick him up and comfort him was so strong that thankfully I did just that, and never went down the controlled crying route, not even for one night. It is so hard to go against what everyone tells you, but boy am I so glad that I did trust my instincts.

It is very hard not to succumb to the pressures of sleep training, because along with the baby expert books, the help lines, and the websites advocating controlled crying, it seems to be the most common form of sleep advice given by health visitors too. If the National Health Service endorses controlled crying, what message are we giving to new mothers? That it is effective? That it is safe? I love this quote from International Board Certified Lactation Consultant Pinky McKay from her article "The Con of Controlled Crying": "Although many sleep 'experts' claim there is no evidence of harm from practices such as controlled crying, it is worth noting that there is a vast difference between '*no evidence of harm*' and '*evidence of NO HARM.*'" It is interesting to note here that Pinky is from Australia, as the Australian Association for Infant Mental Health (AAIMH) states:

> Controlled crying is not consistent with what infants need for their optimal emotional and psychological health, and may have unintended negative consequences. There have been no studies, such as sleep laboratory studies, to our knowledge, that assess the physiological stress levels of infants who undergo controlled crying, or its emotional or psychological impact on the developing child.

While there is evidence that controlled crying works, in that it produces babies who sleep for longer, there is a disturbing lack of evidence into the side effects it may potentially produce. As Pinky McKay says, no evidence of harm caused by controlled crying is most definitely not the same as evidence of it causing no harm.

The Behaviorists and the Rise of the Baby Trainer

Leaving babies to cry for a period of time in order that they may teach themselves to fall asleep or "self-settle," to use the common buzzword of the moment, is actually an old concept introduced by Dr. Emmett Holt in his 1895 book *The Care and Feeding of Children, a Catechism for the Use of Mothers and Children's Nurses.*

This trend continued into the early twentieth century when behavioral psychologist John Watson became president of the American Psychological Association. In this role Watson applied his main theories of behaviorism to parenting and is famous for his warnings to mothers to not give their babies too much love and affection. Watson strongly believed that a baby's behavior and personality could be shaped by the parent and gave strict advice for mothers: "Never hug and kiss them. Never let them sit in your lap. If you must, kiss them once on the forehead when they say goodnight. Shake hands with them in the morning. Give them a pat on the head if they have made an extremely good job of a difficult task."

Behaviorist approaches to the management of sleep issues, such as controlled crying, undoubtedly do work and the results produced are often very quick. The problem lies with how the change is brought about and what other effects it has upon the child. My concerns are summed up nicely by English poet W. H. Auden who said, "Of course, Behaviorism 'works.' So does torture. Give me a no-nonsense, down-to-earth behaviorist, a few drugs, and simple electrical appliances, and in six months I will have him reciting the Athanasian Creed in public."

While Watson was busy advising mothers in America to not smother their babies with love, Truby King was advising similar approaches in New Zealand. He established the Plunket Society, whose mission is "to ensure that New Zealand children are among the healthiest in the world." In his 1942 book *Feeding and Care of Baby*, King highlighted what he saw as the importance of a strict regular routine for babies and how cuddling and too much affection should be avoided in order to build the child's character.

Graduated Extinction

The work of Holt, Watson, and King was further popularized in the 1980s by yet another man, Dr. Richard Ferber, the source of the term "Ferberization." Ferber's book *Solve Your Child's Sleep Problems* became a bestseller with hundreds of thousands of new parents looking to him for advice on how to manage their baby's night waking. Ferber advised that parents follow a routine and that at night they use what he called "graduated extinction" in order to help their baby to sleep through the night. This process required the parent to leave the baby alone in his nursery and then return, at intervals of increasing length, to comfort, without picking him up, the baby's cries. This process should be continued until the baby falls asleep and should be repeated on subsequent nights until the baby falls asleep on his own without adult help.

Ferber has admitted that many misunderstood his work when naming the process of letting a baby cry themselves to sleep as Ferberization and was quoted in an interview with the website Parenting.com as saying, "It's flattering that my name is out there, but it suggests a misunderstanding of what I've been teaching for so long that it concerns me. I've always believed that there are many solutions to sleep problems, and that every family and every child is unique. People want one easy solution, but there's no such thing. I never encouraged parents to let their babies cry it out, but one of the many treatment styles I described in my book is gradual extinction, where you delay your response time to your baby's wakings. I went to great pains in the second edition to clarify that that treatment is not appropriate for every sleep issue, of which there are many. So if someone tells me they tried my 'method,' I know they only read one small part of my book."

A Rose By Any Other Name

Over the past thirty years many babycare authors have picked up on the trend of leaving babies to cry for an increasing period of time with limited physical contact in order to encourage the babies to get themselves to sleep and not wake in the night. Many of these experts claim that their methods are gentle because parents do comfort the baby (perhaps by stroking his forehead, picking him up and putting him down again, ssshing him, or patting his tummy and back) and most choose a new catchy, more gentle sounding name for the process (spaced soothing, pick up put down, controlled calming, and self-soothing are just a handful of examples), but the fact of the matter remains that these methods are not gentle and they do not provide a baby with what they really need, and for the parents, too, these routines are often distressing and anything but gentle.

Does Controlled Crying Work?

While one cannot refute that controlled crying works, it is important to examine what is meant by the above question. Can controlled crying control behavior in much the same way as Watson did almost one hundred years ago? Yes, absolutely it can. Can it result in babies becoming quiet throughout the night? In most cases, yes it can. Can it guarantee a long-term lasting effect? Here the research comes unstuck. In fact it appears that many sleep-trained young babies regress back to regular night waking at around nine months to one year, and I believe there is no small coincidence that this change in wakefulness coincides with the normal psychological occurrence of separation anxiety. Can controlled crying guarantee you a calm, happy, contented baby? It is in answering this question that many scientists around the world would echo a resounding no, for they don't just consider the outcome of a full night's sleep, they also consider *why* controlled crying works.

I believe the advocating of controlled crying by many parenting experts highlights a huge misunderstanding of a young baby's brain and neurophysiological development. Belief in the process of controlled crying relies on a certain set of presumptions, the most concerning of all being that tiny babies can form habits and think logically and rationally, just as an adult does. This presumption is easily dismissed by studying some very basic neuropsychology. When a baby is born its brain is incomplete, first because it is much smaller in size than that of an adult, but also because the vast majority of his brain's 100 billion neurons are not yet connected into networks. What does this mean? The short answer is that babies simply don't think like we do. The neocortex, the part of the brain responsible for logical thinking, does not really spring properly into life until preschool age, so before becoming a toddler a baby's brain is very primal, being focused upon survival and basic emotions, because his most important role as a newborn is survival.

Although a small baby's limited neural capacity influences the way he thinks, early experiences can and do have a big impact on the wiring of an infant's brain. A baby's brain has twice as many synapses, or connections, as he will eventually need. If these synapses are used repeatedly they are reinforced, and if they are not used repeatedly, they are eliminated. This means that we can cause permanent changes in the brain structure of our children, both good and bad, at a very young age. Depriving a baby of the physical contact it needs in infancy can alter the neuroplasticity of its brain, changing the wiring in the relationship part of the brain, which can then affect that child's experience of relationships long into adulthood.[32,33,34,35] Indeed, research on the impact of early attachment confirms that warm, responsive care-giving is essential to healthy brain development and ironically those babies who were allowed to be attached as a baby are those who can truly self-settle as older children and adults. This concept is discussed in more detail in chapter 8.

So why, then, does controlled crying work so effectively at encouraging babies to "sleep through"? The easiest way to answer this is to imagine being upset or hurt yourself. If you were crying and you desperately needed comfort and a big hug from a loved one, imagine how you would feel if they totally ignored you for five or ten minutes, and when they eventually arrived imagine the relief you would feel at seeing them, but hang on, why are they not giving you the hug that you need? Instead they are stroking your brow or patting your tummy? Or, in the case of the "pick up, put down" method they do hug you, but as soon as your wails turn to small sobs they immediately push you away. Now ask yourself, would you bother to keep crying for them? Or would you just give up and retain your hurtful emotions inside?

Imogen O'Reilly, mother of two and blog writer at alternative-mama.com, was so moved by her own perceptions of the experience of a baby undergoing controlled crying she penned the following poem and, while making for a somewhat uncomfortable read, it does make one think more empathically from the baby's point of view:

A letter from a sleep-training baby

Dear mummy,

I am confused.

I am used to falling asleep in your soft, warm arms. Each night I lay snuggled close to you; close enough to hear your heartbeat, close enough to smell your sweet fragrance. I gaze at your beautiful face as I gently drift off to sleep, safe and secure in your loving embrace. When I awaken with a growling stomach, cold feet or because I need a cuddle, you attend to me quickly and before long I am sound asleep once again.

But this last week has been different.

Each night this week has gone like this. You tucked me up into my cot and kissed me goodnight, turned out the light and left. At first I was confused, wondering where you'd gone. Soon I became scared, and called for you. I called and called for you mummy, but you wouldn't come! I was so sad, mummy. I wanted you so badly. I've never felt feelings that strong before. Where did you go?

Eventually you came back! Oh, how happy and re-lieved I was that you came back! I thought you had left me forever! I reached up to you but you wouldn't pick me up. You wouldn't even look me in the eye. You lay me back down with those soft warm arms, said 'shh, it's night time now' and left again.

This happened again, over and over. I screamed for you and after a while, longer each time, you would return but you wouldn't hold me.

After I had screamed a while, I had to stop. My throat hurt so badly. My head was pounding and my tiny tummy was growling. My heart hurt the most, though. I just couldn't understand why you wouldn't come.

After what felt like a lifetime of nights like this, I gave up. You don't come when I scream, and when you do finally come you won't even look me in the eye, let alone hold my shaking, sobbing little body. The screaming hurt too much to carry on for very long.

I just don't understand, mummy. In the daytime when I fall and bump my head, you pick me up and kiss it better. If I am hungry, you feed me. If I crawl over to you for a cuddle, you read my mind and scoop me up, covering my tiny face with kisses and telling me how special I am and how much you love me. If I need you, you respond to me straight away.

But at night time, when it's dark and quiet and my nightlight casts strange shadows on my wall, you disappear. I can see that you're tired; mummy, but I love you so much. I just want to be near to you, that's all.

Now, at night time, I am quiet. But I still miss you.

The Risks of Controlled Crying

Another way to understand why controlled crying might work is to look at American psychologist Martin Seligman's theory of learned helplessness and apply it to human babies. In 1965, while researching the relationship between fear and learning in dogs, Seligman harnessed the dogs so that they were unable to move and then rang a bell while giving them an electric shock. Next, Seligman removed the harnesses from the dogs, which meant that they were now physically able to move out of the way of the electric shock, and rang the bell again. The dogs however did not move, despite being able to jump out of the way of the shock; they had learned to be helpless and did not even try to avoid the painful stimulation. The dogs had learned it was futile trying to get away from the shocks, so why try? How is this applicable to a baby undergoing controlled crying? Why does he stop calling out? Could it be because it is futile for him to continue crying? Why cry when nobody comes?

The Negative Consequences

The potential negative consequences of controlled crying are many. They may include the following:

- Babies miss out on stimulating touch from their parents, which we know is important for them to thrive. (See chapter 8.)
- Babies may not receive adequate nutrition throughout the night and, if the mother is breastfeeding, controlled crying may have implications, including negatively affecting milk supply.[36]
- Babies suffer from increased cortisol levels which may lead to neurological damage.[37,38,39,40,41,42] When a baby continuously secretes cortisol as an infant it can have an effect on their stress response in later life, as they may either over- or under-produce cortisol when stressed as an adult. Either of these is undesirable as too much cortisol can lead to anxiety and depression and too little can lead to ambivalence and emotional detachment.
- Babies may suffer from increased pulse, blood pressure, and temperature.
- Babies may vomit during the process; amazingly some baby trainers consider this to be the baby protesting about the sleep training and say to ignore it!

- As we have just seen, possible learned helplessness phenomenon.
- Potential negative effects on secure attachment.

With all of this in mind I find it shocking that so many experts still recommend controlled crying as the "gold standard" in solving baby sleep problems. Indeed it is suggested[43] that a massive 61 percent of parenting books available in America endorse it. The persistent popularity of this method in the last hundred years is a topic that frequently perplexes many psychologists,[44] particularly in the face of new research suggesting that very real physical changes happen to a baby when undergoing controlled crying. Recent research[45] has shown that while only initially stressful to a mother for the first couple of days when the baby is crying a lot, controlled crying continues to have a negative physiological effect, in the form of raised cortisol levels, on the baby afterwards, even when he stops crying and appears content. Speaking from the baby's point of view the researchers commented, "They no longer expressed behavioral distress during the sleep transition but their cortisol levels were elevated."

This problem may be even more pronounced when we consider the earlier discussion of neuroplasticity and the possibility that some of the baby's cortisol receptors may be deleted in response to these episodes through a lack of reinforcement. What impact might this have on the child in the future? This is an issue discussed by psychotherapist Sue Gerhardt in her book *Why Love Matters: How Affection Shapes a Baby's Brain*: "a brain well stocked with cortisol receptors through this early experience will be better able to mop up this stress hormone when it is released in future. This furnishes the baby's brain with the capacity to stop producing cortisol when it has helped deal with a source of stress. The stress response will be quickly turned off when it is no longer needed."

The wise words of pediatrician Dr. Paul Fleiss, taken from his book *Sweet Dreams: A Pediatrician's Secrets for Your Child's Good Night's Sleep* sum up the issue of controlled crying:

The idea, often heard these days, that babies can and should learn to "self-soothe," without any physical or emotional interaction with parents, is incorrect. The best and most effective way for a child to learn to lull himself quietly back to sleep after experiencing a night waking is for parents to have demonstrated their dependability and availability when the child was a baby. Otherwise, that emotional upset the baby suffered as a result of the traumatic event that aroused him from sleep in the first place may be compounded by the terror and frustration of feeling abandoned and unwanted. If a baby learns that his mother will come to him whenever he awakens in distress and cries out for her, he is more likely to develop into a self-reliant and self-assured child who will have the ability to assess and manage his own night wakings without involving his parents unnecessarily. It cannot be overly stressed that depriving a baby or a child of emotional support when he needs or wants it runs the risk of creating an emotionally unstable child and eventually an emotionally unstable adult. Only good can come from cuddling your baby whenever he needs it.

The Alternatives

So what does all of this research mean for the sleep-deprived parents of the world? Does it mean that you must cope with any amount of exhaustion thrown at you? That you should not complain about or try to change your baby's sleep behavior, no matter how much they may wake at night? Should you soldier on, even though you are worried about the effect the sleepless nights are having upon your bonding with your baby and your emotional wellbeing?

The answer is, of course not. As I said right at the very beginning of this book, you matter too. I often hear the phrase "happy mom = happy baby" bandied around by the controlled crying advocates and there is some truth in that. My main issues, however, are (1) Are the moms REALLY happy? Or is the controlled crying making them feel sad? (2) There is much more to a happy baby and a happy mom than sleeping through the night, and (3) It is possible to have a positive influence on a baby's sleep without having to resort to controlled crying. Indeed, some of these other techniques can even aid bonding, improve breastfeeding (if that is how you have chosen to feed your baby), and help to calm moms as well as babies. What I'm saying here is that you do have options. It isn't as cut and dried as "controlled cry or be a martyr and wait it out." There are lots of things you can do that will help, gently, and we'll discuss these in the next chapter.

Tracey's Story

Liberty had always been what many would call a clingy baby. She loved to be with me all the time, didn't cope with strangers too well, and just wanted to be wherever I was, bedtime included. After a long period of time with me mostly, and my husband when it all got a bit too much, sitting by the side of her crib stroking her until she fell asleep, only to have to do it again if she woke during the night, we decided enough was enough. We felt we needed some evenings to ourselves, some "us" time back, and it couldn't be good for Liberty either to be getting less and less sleep.

At the time, I also frequently used an online parenting forum, so asked the advice of other moms on there. The words "controlled crying" were mentioned time and time again. "OK," they said, "it's not for everyone and it is gut wrenching but it works and quickly!" Hmmm, the gut wrenching part didn't quite sit comfortably with me, but I was so tired with such a painful back from sitting for up to two hours in my daughter's room at night that I was willing to try an alternative.

We researched online and found that the method in question was covered in a book by Richard Ferber—*Solve Your Child's Sleep Problems*. It promised to solve any issues within a few days, so the book was swiftly ordered. Before the book arrived and while I was reading through it to gain an understanding of how to do this properly, we embarked on more of a routine at bedtime and ensured that every night included bath, feed while reading a story, and bed, so that Liberty knew what to expect every night.

The day arrived when we were going to start with the controlled crying. I distinctly remember it was a Friday night, as the plan was by Monday and return to work, we would have a settled child at bedtime and we would get an evening to ourselves too! The recommended intervals for returning the first night were three, five, then every ten minutes until Liberty fell asleep but I didn't feel comfortable with that so we decided just to go up in two-minute increments to a maximum of eight minutes.

I kissed Liberty goodnight that first night with a huge fixed smile on my face to cover my anxiety, told her to be a good girl and I'd see her in the morning. She smiled back then I quickly left the room. I barely made it down the stairs before she started screaming and crying. It was absolutely awful, as I somehow knew it would be, but I sat with my husband on the sofa listening to the baby monitor and it felt like an eternity until that two minutes was up so I could go back. I then went back up, laid her back down whispering, "It's night time now," and rubbed her back a bit.

I didn't want to leave again as tears were rolling down her face but I had to. I think she cried for almost an hour that first night before the monitor finally went silent, but in that time she was sick with crying so much. As was suggested, I had to go up and clean her up and change the bed but not make a fuss. I had to have a quick cuddle and kiss before putting her back to bed again; mother instinct kicked in, I think. Well, we had done it, but it felt like a rather hollow achievement somehow. When I went up to check on her, she lay hot and sticky with her hair stuck to her face, and I felt pretty sad.

The next night followed the same way to begin with, with Liberty right straight away but, lo and behold, 20 minutes later the monitor was silent; a much less stressful experience than the night before thankfully. The third night saw almost complete success, as she whimpered and cried for a couple of minutes before self-settling. The book recommends following the program for two to seven days and there's no denying it does work eventually, but I feel guilty that we put our daughter through it when all she was doing by crying was communicating with us that she wanted to be with us. We should have just accepted that. Having also read evidence of the possible long-term effects of leaving a baby to cry for long periods, I do feel truly guilty and really regret it.

When my second child Noah came along, I managed to breastfeed for a longer period of time than with my daughter. Every naptime and bedtime he was fed to sleep, so yet again, once he was around a year old, we had the same problem. He wouldn't go to bed without a feed and would wake several times in the night and of course needed to be fed back to sleep each time, pretty much making my husband redundant and me very exhausted. It all got a bit too much once again one night, resulting in us sitting down to discuss what to do next. My husband briefly mentioned trying controlled crying again, but I knew that I couldn't go there again. I wanted a gentle approach to help Noah self-soothe, which wouldn't cause so much heartache all around. Granted it took longer, probably around a month, but it was a much calmer learning curve for us all. It was so much better.

I think, in conclusion, a mother must make an informed choice after reading the literature supported by the evidence and, if not, trust their own instinct. I wish I had the first time around.

Chapter 7

Ten Ways to Encourage More Sleep at Night

The best bridge between despair and hope is a good night's sleep.

—E. Joseph Cossman, businessman and entrepreneur

Lots of new moms ask me if there is anything they can do to help their baby to sleep a little longer at night without resorting to controlled crying. It is something I was also desperate to know as a new mother myself, but it is hard to find help that doesn't fall into one of the following varieties:

Well, he probably needs weaning, he's a big boy, and he's nearly sixteen weeks old; just give him a bit of baby rice.

Try topping him up with hungry baby milk just before you go to bed; he's probably hungry.

If you let him cry a bit rather than always picking him up he will learn to get himself off to sleep and that's what you need—self-settling.

Buy some black-out curtains and make sure you have the same bedtime every night, always put him down awake, and never, ever let him fall asleep in your arms.

As it happens, when I was a new mother I tried all the methods. My firstborn finally slept through when he was about six months old. Now at ten years old, though, he takes ages to get to sleep, is always asking for more hugs, more kisses, another drink, door open, lights left on, any excuse to not go to bed alone—he has been this way since he turned twelve months old, after an all-too-short interlude of quiet nights and easy bedtimes. He also shows some of the issues potentially caused by weaning too soon, as mentioned in chapter 6.[46,47,48]

Baby- and Parent-Friendly Ways to Encourage More Sleep

In this chapter I will be discussing a few of the methods that can help you and your baby to get more sleep without resorting to early weaning and controlled crying. I have to reiterate before I go on that, for me, having realistic expectations of my babies' sleep was probably the most reassuring thing to learn. I finish this chapter by looking at co-sleeping, perhaps one of the best ways to encourage more sleep for all of you!

Listen to Your Baby

A while ago, one of the new moms from my antenatal classes phoned me and we had a long chat about her beautiful home water-birth. She told me she had bonded instantly with her daughter, the breastfeeding was going really well, and for the most part she was really enjoying her time with her new baby. At the time her baby was about eight weeks old. She had one big problem and that was her real reason for calling me. "Sarah, her sleeping is awful, I don't know what to do, can you help me?"

I asked her if she could explain what she meant by her daughter's sleep being awful and she replied, "Well she will always go to sleep during a feed and she'll sleep in my arms for ages, but the minute I put her into her Moses basket, she screams and screams and screams." I asked her what happened if she didn't put her down. The new mom replied, "Oh yes, she likes that, she'll sleep pretty much all night, she just hates her basket." I asked how she felt about not moving her to her basket, perhaps by using a sling in the day and bed sharing at night.

Her reply was, "Oh I wouldn't mind, I love having her close to me, but my mom and health visitor say she has to learn to sleep alone and that if I don't put her down her sleep will be awful as she'll learn bad sleep habits." The two of them went on to become avid fans of babywearing and shared a bed peacefully for the next two years. Funnily enough her baby's sleep problem went away too, once she listened. Babies may not speak, but they are excellent at communicating their needs. Maybe we should try listening to them?

Trust Your Instinct

I still remember vividly the wonder of sitting up in bed, snuggling next to my small baby and feeding in the wee hours. We would often drift off to sleep together and I would then awake with a great start and feeling of horror, worrying that I should put him back in his crib. Invariably, when I moved to put him down he would either begin hungrily suckling again or cry voraciously if I put him down. I would then sit for hours rocking his crib from side to side, making shushing noises, singing lullabies, and stroking his forehead.

If that didn't work my husband would pace the hallway with him, back and forth, back and forth. On bad nights he used to buckle Seb into his car seat and drive him backwards and forwards up and down our driveway to encourage him to nod off, while on really bad nights he used to drive around the village in his pajamas and robe for hours on end. If only I had trusted my instincts and not the books I had read, or the warnings that well-meaning friends and health professionals had given me, I may not have ever felt the need to repeatedly ignore my feelings and put him back in his crib, which in turn may well have resulted in calmer, more peaceful nights full of slumber for us all. This was something this mother also experienced:

> The first was hardest. I wasn't used to the lack of sleep. I also didn't know it was OK to co-sleep. With my second baby, my husband was working away and I was left with two under two. I went with my gut, threw out the baby books, and pulled my daughter into my bed. Breastfeeding became much easier and I got more sleep to cope with my toddler during the day. She eventually moved on to become our best sleeper and started sleeping through a good core night by seven months. Our third was in our bed from the get-go because I knew how different it was for me stress wise. If I can get a good night's rest the whole family is better off.

Knowing What Is Coming Next

We can actually use our knowledge of behaviorism from the last chapter to help us come up with gentler ways of settling babies. Babies definitely do learn from an early age, but not in the same way as adults, as their learning is much more simplistic. What they do learn quickly is an expectation of what comes next. I quickly learned that if I bathed my baby in deep, warm water, massaged him on a rug in his room, and then fed him in a rocking chair with only a dim lamp for light he would inevitably drift off to sleep. It seemed he had learned to expect that bath + massage + low light + food = bed and sleep. While we had no routine in the daytime in terms of naps and feeding, apart from the natural patterns he followed himself, I kept to the same ritual in the evening. We didn't always bathe him, but I would always massage him, change him into a different onesie, and then sit down to feed in dim light.

The benefit of this type of ritual, as opposed to a strict routine, is that it is portable; wherever you are you can carry out the same ritual as it does not require strict timings or specific nursery equipment. Add to this research[49,50,51] that shows that baby massage alone helps babies to fall to sleep faster and stay asleep for longer, our little ritual became a powerful sleep trigger.

Conditioning and Cues

Again, using a positive application of behavioral theories, I added two further cues to our bedtime ritual: smell and sound.

For the smell I purchased a battery operated aromatherapy fan (the batteries were important as I wanted it to be mobile and couldn't always guarantee the use of a plug socket, particularly on vacation) and added one drop of chamomile and one drop of lavender essential oil each evening while we massaged and fed. I made sure I always used the same oils, both known for their soothing, calming, and sleep-inducing properties, in order that the link between them, relaxation, and sleep was as strong as possible.

For the sound I bought a relaxing instrumental CD, which I played at the same time throughout the massage, cuddles, and feed, every single night. The smell and the music became equally strong cues and even at age four my children would go right back to sleep when their music was played at night. If they were finding it hard to sleep, particularly when they were teething or sick, the smell did wonders to calm them and soothe them to sleep.

This approach works particularly wonderfully on vacation when everything is new to a baby, but they still have the reassuring triggers of home. Remember that they must always be conditioned first. In other words, don't expect a music CD or essential oil to work magic alone; you have to teach your baby "this smell" = calm and "this music" = calm. You have to work with the association, and it will take time to build. The results will not be instant as with controlled crying, but you will notice a difference in time.

Comforters

I think people often misunderstand comforters as being items for babies to cuddle and calm themselves with by touch, but I have always believed the most important thing about comforters (for my firstborn it was simply a knotted muslin with a silky label he liked to feel) is the smell, most importantly the smell of the mother. In the book *The Social Baby* by Lynne Murray there are some amazing photos of newborns turning towards breastpads that had been in their mothers' bras, and which had thus picked up her scent, and ignoring those that had not. Smell is vitally important to the feeding and bonding of all mammals; we are no different!

English pediatrician and psychoanalyst Donald Winnicott refers to comfort objects as "mother substitutes" and believes them to be an important bridge between dependence and independence. I don't think they are important for all babies, and some babies don't need them at all, but they can be very helpful if you need to take a bit of a break sometimes or leave your baby with someone else for a short time before they may be ready to leave you, and they can be very useful for helping your baby to still remain close to you, through scent, during the night. If you want to use a comforter I recommend a cotton fabric, which can easily absorb your scent. You could try putting the comforter in your bra for the day and it will absorb your smell and comfort your baby even more.

If you do want to use a comforter with your baby, I can't stress how important it is to buy more than one. I speak from experience when I say how stressful it is to suddenly realize you have lost a beloved comforter and have no way of replacing it. My son lost his "blanky" that I had purchased, one of a kind, from America. No amount of searching revealed a replacement and we had a very unhappy couple of weeks when he refused to sleep without it.

Swaddling

If your baby is still very little and you don't feel co-sleeping is for you, swaddling can work magic for encouraging sleep. It works in three ways: (1) to help the baby still feel as if he is being held by you; (2) by inhibiting the startle (Moro) reflex; and (3) by keeping your baby snug and warm. There are always a few safety rules to bear in mind when swaddling (as mentioned in chapter 3) and if you are breastfeeding always make sure that the feeding is well established before swaddling. Don't forget to give your baby lots of skin-to-skin contact too; adding swaddling to the end of your bath–massage–feed routine can work really well.

Daddy Cuddles

On nights when I was truly exhausted and my babies were just that little bit older I used to sleep in our spare room and leave the baby in bed with my husband, still cuddled, still responded to as soon as they cried, but not straight on the breast. I only advocate this very occasionally if the mom really is exhausted and needs to catch up on sleep.

Breastfeeding to Calm

Something else that helped us, particularly with my last baby who still wanted to suckle at least four times through the night at twelve months, was to allow her free access to the breast whenever she wanted (denying her seemed to make her more fervent in her search), but to de-latch her once she was calm and just starting to drift off to sleep. She knew she could always have the breast whenever she wanted, but that it was not for going to sleep with; it was simply for getting calm. I think at some point something clicked when she realized she could feed whenever she wanted in the night, but not to actually go to sleep, so she seemed to be far less interested. This is most definitely a tip for older babies only, though; I would suggest once they are at least six months or older.

Sleep Breeds Sleep

Quite a few people used to say, "Sleep breeds sleep" to me when I first became a mother and I never really understood what they meant, but now I do. I was discussing my non-sleeping six-month-old with a midwife friend and she said, "Sarah, do you think you maybe do too much with him? He might be overtired." This shook me as I did everything in my power to fill our days with activities, thinking that the more I did the more tired he would be and the better his sleep would be. We did baby yoga, baby swimming, baby music, baby signing, baby dancing, coffee mornings, and baby groups. I used to do at least one activity a day, sometimes two, and I thought it helped; I thought I tired him out (goodness knows I was tired!).

I decided to try an experiment; I had a week of staying at home, lots of cuddles, going for quiet walks, just day-to-day general life and chores, and the resulting change in his behavior surprised me. He slept better than he had for months and not only that, he was calmer too. With my younger three we did barely any groups and classes and they each slept significantly better. Is that a coincidence?

I am often shocked at the packed social lives of babies and can't help wondering how difficult all of the stimulation must be for such tiny little things. I always stress the importance of calming the parent in my classes too—adrenaline is catching. In order to have a calm, sleepy baby we must first have a calm parent!

Co-Sleeping and Bed Sharing

Sleeping with your baby in your bed can be one of the most wonderful ways for you all to enjoy a peaceful night's sleep, but the concept is shrouded in myth and mystery.

I decided to investigate the incidence of co-sleeping, having commonly seen figures of 60 or 70 percent bandied around. Several research studies indicate the range to be somewhere between 40 and 80 percent, dependent on many factors including ethnicity, age of parent, and age of baby. So I ran my own mini survey, which elicited 250 replies from mothers in the UK.

I asked simply, "Have you ever slept in the same bed as your baby?" A huge 92 percent answered with a resounding "yes." Then I asked if they would mind sharing their reasons for co-sleeping and these are just some of the responses I received:

> We chose to co-sleep because our first child wouldn't sleep longer than 45 minutes in his Moses basket. After trying and failing to get him into a routine we decided it was best for our sanity to have him in the bed especially since I was breastfeeding. We co-slept until he was eight months. Now our daughter has arrived we didn't even try to put her in a crib/Moses basket; she was straight in our bed and she sleeps for four hours at night which means all of us get a good night's sleep.

> My baby sleeps well both on her own and in bed with us. We don't co-sleep every night; usually it's after her 3 AM feed when we keep her in bed with us the rest of the night. So I guess you could say it's modified co-sleeping because she starts out in her crib. She doesn't seem to mind either arrangement but I love having her near me, which I never thought would be the case. Before I had her, I was absolutely against co-sleeping and swore I would never do it.

Our twin boys are our first babies. We have a co-sleeper crib [for more on these, see below], so we planned to co-sleep from the beginning. We suspected it would be easier for my recovery and more comforting for the boys. The bed sharing was a bit of a surprise to us. It happened in response to lack of sleep, probably. It continued because it felt natural to us. We only stopped bed sharing regularly at seven months when the boys became so active we couldn't safely keep them in bed with us. (The monkeys crawl right for the edge every time they wake in the night.)

The bond is amazing. We both sleep better when co-sleeping, and the sleep apnea [breath holding] issues that my little one has don't happen when he is in the bed with me; we have found that while in the bed with me he gets in sync with my breathing pattern.

When he was first born he would not sleep on his own, so we started bringing him in bed with us in order to get some sleep! Now he is six months and has slept in his own crib for a while now, but still comes in bed with us after an early morning feed (6 AM-ish).

Initially, it felt right. I just couldn't imagine leaving my tiny baby on his own in a room in the dark all night. That felt really unnatural and wrong to me. As a bonus, I get so much more sleep.

[We did it] because it is far easier for breastfeeding at night and much better for both mother and baby to be close when sleeping. My children are now five and eight and regularly come and get into bed with us if they wake up early in the morning. Or indeed in the middle of the night! I think a family all sleeping together sometimes is a really nice, cozy thing to do, even if the children are watching TV while the parents attempt to sleep . . .

I believe that it is best for our baby and for us. I did a lot of research before she was born and realized that the literature which presents the "risks" of co-sleeping is flawed in that it often does not distinguish between intentional and accidental co-sleeping. We have worked to create a safe sleeping environment (plenty of space, safe bedding, etc.) and are conscious of the risk factors (e.g., no alcohol). Co-sleeping ensures we all get a better night's sleep even through growth spurts as I can breast-feed my baby as soon as she needs it; she doesn't need to get upset in order to get my attention and neither of us has to wake up 100 percent so it's easier to get back to sleep! Having a family bed also helps bonding between father and baby as they get more time close to each other despite him being out at work all day—she usually falls asleep holding his finger.

It felt beautiful and completely normal for me and my baby. He was happy and I was happy. We both slept well. It made life easy. I also felt entirely confident in following my instincts.

Why keep getting up out of bed for night feeds when I can have all-night snuggles instead?

With my first, my instincts told me this was how my baby and I should sleep at night. I was a bit nervous about do-ing it so struggled along for a while, sometimes falling asleep on the sofa with him during night feeds! I was ex-hausted, nothing comforted him like being with me, and I soon realized I was being silly "fighting" it and far better and safer to embrace what I knew was right for us. I appeased my worries by reading up on how to do it safely.

I breastfed both children and I am too lazy to get out of a warm cozy bed to feed; easier to lie on my side, feed, and then fall back to sleep . . . given that breastfeeding reduces the risk of SIDS by roughly one-third and I had no other independent risk factors I didn't view it as "risky." Some of the lowest rates of SIDS are to be found in cultures where co-sleeping is the norm.

I waited fifteen years for her and could not be apart from her. Eight IVFs can do funny things to you.

Avoiding the Risks of Sharing a Bed with Your Baby

In my survey I also asked whether the mother was aware of the potential risks associated with sleeping in the same bed as your baby (namely overlaying, rolling onto your baby, and resulting suffocation risks). Ninety-eight percent replied "yes." Naturally, then, I asked whether they were aware of how to reduce these risks; this time 95 percent replied "yes," leaving 5 percent who share a bed with their baby unaware of how to reduce these risks. This is a small percentage, but 5 percent more than I would like to see.

The following list explains how to reduce the potential risks of bed sharing:

1. Ideally only bed share if you are breastfeeding (breastfeeding mothers have a heightened sense of awareness to their babies and are therefore less likely to roll onto their baby, and more likely to assume a protective "cradling" position around their baby), as breastfeeding in itself also offers protection against sudden infant death syndrome (SIDS).

2. Always carefully plan your sleeping environment and only ever sleep with your baby in a bed, never a sofa, beanbag, or similar. Ensure that the bed's mattress is firm and that pillows, blankets, and duvets are kept well out of the way of your baby to avoid the risk of suffocation. Make sure that the room is not too warm.

3. Carefully plan the position of yourself and your baby. You should always sleep between your baby and partner; never put the baby in the middle of the bed, as your partner does not have the same protective instincts against rolling onto your baby as you do; and ensure your baby is positioned in the crook of your arm—well below your pillows. Your body should form a protective "frame" all around your baby with you on your side (see the illustration below). Never sleep with your baby lying on your chest as there is a risk he or she may roll off. Always check that your baby cannot get trapped between the bed and the wall or in the side of a bed-guard (if you use one). Ideally the bed will be low to the floor, like a futon, or a mattress directly on the floor. You can also buy special co-sleeping cribs and special bed-guards designed for co-sleeping families to prevent your baby from falling out of the bed or getting trapped between the bed and the wall (see box opposite).

4. Never share a bed with your baby if you or your partner smokes.

5. Never share a bed with your baby if you or your partner has consumed alcohol.

6. Never share a bed with your baby if you are taking prescription or recreational drugs.

7. Never share a bed with your baby if you are overtired/ exhausted.

8. Remove any necklaces, tie your hair up, and don't wear night-clothes with ties that could present choking hazards to your baby.

9. Never share a bed with your baby if they are unwell or have a fever.

10. Do not share a bed with your baby if they were born pre-mature or with a low birth weight.

Co-Sleeper Cribs

Co-sleeper cribs provide a separate sleeping surface that attaches to the parents' bed, allowing for an independent sleeping situation for the baby with easy access for feeding and comforting. Further information is available from www.armsreach.com. Another alternative is to adapt a regular drop-side crib by removing the drop side. Or there is the Humanity Co-sleeper, which is a special pad and bumper to stop the baby falling out of the bed. See www. humanityorganics.com.

Many healthcare professionals and publications strongly advise against sharing a bed with your baby and indeed the Foundation for the Study of Infant Deaths (FSID) advises parents that: "The safest place for your baby to sleep is in a crib or cot in a room with you for the first six months." My personal viewpoint is that all parents should be supported in their choices, and that those choices should be informed. If a parent wishes to sleep with their baby in their bed, then I strongly believe that health professionals have a duty to help them to do this as safely as possible. Indeed we already know that around 60 percent of all new parents do share a bed with their baby at some point and most do this in secret, feeling guilty for doing so and confessing in whispers that they do it. These parents are still sleeping with their babies despite all the advice not to, so to me it makes infinitely more sense to help those parents to understand how to minimize risk as much as possible.

I must confess to having a strong bias here, as I firmly believe bed sharing saved my daughter's life. One night, when my daughter was around two months old I awoke to find her still and blue in the crook of my arm. She had stopped breathing. Instinctively I shook her and blew in her face and to my great relief she gasped and began to breathe again. I have no idea for how long she had stopped breathing or what would have happened if I had not woken and stimulated her to breathe, and it doesn't bear thinking about. All I know is that if she had been anywhere but in my arms then I doubt I would have been jolted awake with a feeling that something was not OK. Did bed sharing save her life? I don't know, but I am so very grateful we shared a bed that night.

Bed Sharing Myths and Misunderstandings

Many myths abound about co-sleeping. Critics say that it is dangerous, that it will create clingy children who will never learn independence, and that it is weird and unnatural. Falling asleep with your baby can indeed be very dangerous. Sleeping with a baby on a sofa, sharing a bed with a baby if you smoke, sharing a bed with your baby if you have consumed alcohol, sharing a bed with your baby if you have taken prescription medication, sharing a bed with your baby if you are overtired— yes, all of these things are dangerous and MUST be avoided . . . but sharing a bed with your baby following the simple rules already mentioned is not dangerous. In fact there have been no studies that show the dangers of co-sleeping when following the rules I listed above.

Even the most recent research[52] used to illustrate the dangers of bed sharing suggests that planned bed sharing carries no increased risk to babies, with the researchers commenting on their findings: "Routine bed sharing did not increase the risk of SIDS. However, bed sharing during the last night [the night before the crib death occurred] when bed sharing was not routine increased the risk two-fold."

Added to this, much of the research quoted to prove how dangerous bed sharing is has many flaws. The research is often full of confounding variables, meaning that the researchers have overlooked many subtle points and activities that could skew the results, which means that the results of the study become unreliable and lose their replicability and thus become largely invalid—these factors are the holy trinity of clinical research, and without them one cannot draw any conclusions from the study results.

At this moment in time nobody can categorically say "bed sharing is dangerous." It is naive at best and deceiving at worst to use negative studies to tell parents not to sleep with their babies. To quote Dr. William Sears:

> Until a legitimate survey is done to determine how many babies sleep with their parents, and this is factored into the rate of SIDS in a bed versus a crib, it is unwarranted to state that sleeping in a crib is safer than a bed. If the incidence of SIDS is dramatically higher in crib versus a parent's bed, and because the cases of accidental smothering and entrapment are only 1.5% of the total SIDS cases, then sleeping with a baby in your bed would be far safer than putting baby in a crib. The answer is not to tell parents they shouldn't sleep with their baby, but rather to educate them on how to sleep with their infants safely.

You'll Never Get That Baby Out of Your Bed!

Safety fears allayed, we are hit with the next wall, the nay-sayers who tell us, "It's not good for the baby; they need to learn independence."

My answer is an overwhelming, yes, they do, but before independence first comes dependence. When a baby is born they need us; they cannot survive without us, indeed they do not even realize they are a separate entity to us until they are about three months old. So much research (which we will look at in the next chapter) speaks about the importance of infant attachment, the baby–carer bond, and how if an infant is allowed to be as attached to their parent as they need then we can help to create a confident toddler, child, and adult. Separating a baby from its parent before it is ready to separate does not make the baby autonomous or independent; it deprives the infant of a basic need.

Or how about those who say co-sleeping is bad for marriages, and that the baby comes between man and wife, literally. One of the biggest causes of relationship breakdown is stress, so if you imagine the stress of a non-sleeping baby night after night, and contrast that with the thought of a baby sleeping peacefully at night, albeit in your bed—which one do you think would make you more stressed and thus impact on your relationship with your partner the most? I believe that co-sleeping can frequently do the opposite and save relationships!

Bed Sharing around the World

In many countries around the world co-sleeping is the cultural norm, but the most interesting example in relation to the SIDS debate is the Far East. During the 1990s in Japan the SIDS rate was only one-tenth of that of the West and in Hong Kong it was only 3 percent, so what is the difference between Western society and that of Japan and Hong Kong? Co-sleeping is normal in Japan and Hong Kong! Recent research has also shown us that the parenting practices of other cultures impact on risks that could influence SIDS rates. For example, anthropologists from Durham University's Sleep Lab[53] recently compared parenting practices and SIDS rates between white British families and those of Pakistani origin, and found that babies of Pakistani origin were significantly more likely to sleep in their parents' bed than babies of white British origin. The Pakistani parents were also less likely to smoke, drink alcohol, and sofa share, all of which are known risk factors for SIDS, than their white British counterparts. Consider the possibility, then, that our relatively high SIDS risk could even be lowered if we followed the Pakistani example of co-sleeping—that's quite something, isn't it!

There are other factors, too, which potentially mean it is safer for your baby to sleep in your bed than alone, including the concepts of limbic regulation and gaseous exchange (see box) and the decreased levels of infant apnea (breath holding) found when a baby is near their mother.[54] Add to this the increased arousability

Limbic Regulation And Gaseous Exchange

Limbic regulation is a remarkable natural phenomenon whereby a mother appears to be neurologically and chemically in sync with her baby, and her baby with her. We have seen that research shows us that the sleep cycles of a mother and baby sharing a bed are intertwined and synchronised.[55] Indeed, further research[56] shows us that a mother's body acts to regulate that of her baby, perhaps through helping to increase a cool body temperature or regulate breathing patterns.

Gaseous exchange is a term used to describe the process of breathing, exchanging oxygen and carbon dioxide between body and atmosphere. When used in relation to a mother and baby sharing a bed, gaseous exchange can be taken a step further, whereby the mother's exhalation of carbon dioxide may be seen to prompt the baby to breath to take in oxygen, potentially ensuring that an infant's respiration remains steady and reducing incidences of apnea (breath holding).[57,58,59] in breastfeeding moms, which results in a heightened awareness of their baby, and we have to wonder whether we are ignoring the great wisdom of evolution by keeping our babies away from us at night.

Bed sharing can also mean more sleep for everyone. Time and again, research[60] has shown that, contrary to popular opinion, bed sharing mothers get more sleep than those with crib sleeping babies. Much of this research is led by the anthropologist Professor James McKenna, head of the University of Notre Dame Mother–Baby Behavioral Sleep Laboratory in Indiana. Along with other researchers, namely those from Durham University's Sleep Lab as previously mentioned, McKenna has also studied closely the correlations between breastfeeding and bed sharing. In his words:

> Bed sharing makes breastfeeding much easier to manage and practically doubles the amount of breastfeeding sessions while permitting both mothers and infants to spend more time asleep. The increased exposure to mother's antibodies which comes with more frequent night-time breastfeeding can potentially, per any given infant, reduce infant illness. And because co-sleeping in the form of bed sharing makes breastfeeding easier for mothers, it encourages them to breastfeed for a greater number of months . . . therein potentially reducing the mother's chances of breast cancer. Indeed, the benefits of co-sleeping helps explain why simply telling parents never to sleep with baby is like suggesting that nobody should eat fats and sugars since excessive fats and sugars lead to obesity and/or death from heart disease, diabetes, or cancer. Obviously, there's a whole lot more to the story.

Finally, the benefits of bed sharing also include better parent–child bonding.[61,62]

All of this considered, please do not think that by pointing out all of the benefits of sharing a bed with your baby I am trying to persuade you to sleep with your baby in your bed; I am merely trying to correct some of the misinformation that abounds in society concerning co-sleeping. Just in case it is something you think you might like to do, but are too scared, or perhaps it is something you have done accidentally—when you have fallen asleep in a chair or in bed at night while feeding your baby—and woke feeling guilty for the risks you had exposed them to. Bed sharing isn't for everyone, but for those for whom it is instinctively right I believe it is really important that they are taught how to do it as safely as possible and are reassured that they are not damaging their baby either physically or psychologically—in fact quite the reverse could be true.

Bed Sharing When The Second Baby Arrives

When your second baby arrives, if your first is still bed sharing with you and you're happy with that, why not keep on with the arrangement? Just make sure you sleep between the toddler and the new baby. Or, you could try the following:

- Toddler stays in the bed and the new baby sleeps in a co-sleeper crib/sidecar alongside the big bed.
- Toddler moves to a mattress on the floor next to the big bed.
- Dad sleeps with the toddler, while mom sleeps with the new baby. (While dads shouldn't sleep beside newborns it's OK for them to sleep beside a toddler.)
- Toddler moves into his own crib/bed well before the baby is born.

Charlotte's Story

I remember sitting on my sofa holding my gorgeous baby boy just a day and half old. . . . The midwife shuffled her papers and looked up and announced that she was now going to tell me how to sleep with my baby safely! Sleep with my baby!!!! Was she mad? I didn't want to kill him. . . . I had heard all the horror stories of babies dying by being suffocated in bed. So why was this midwife going to advise me on how to sleep with him? I declined her advice exclaiming that I was NEVER going to co-sleep. She ignored my protest and told me that at some stage as I breastfed my tiny baby in the middle of the night I would fall asleep. I listened. She was right . . .

The first time I fell asleep with him cocooned in my arms, my body curled around him creating a protective wall. . . . I woke with a start, horrified that I had fallen asleep with him in bed. But a funny thing happened . . . it felt strangely all right. He slept soundly; I slept soundly; my husband slept soundly. Had I just discovered the secret to actually getting some sleep?

Over the coming nights and weeks we flitted between him sleeping with me and then going back into his Moses basket next to my bed as I thought it was the right thing to do; well I wouldn't want to make a "rod for my own back" now would I?

But my instincts and arms cried out to hold him and cradle him all night. So I did. I was a breastfeeding mom; I know all the "safe sleeping" advice and thoroughly enjoyed sleeping with him; and so did my husband. He was getting a good night's sleep and the floorboards ceased being walked at 3 AM.

My little boy recently turned two and all I hear is "Arthur do it, Arthur do it" whenever I try and do anything for him. He loves sleeping like a star fish and I have made no rod for my own back. I have precious memories, a confident little boy who has received so many cuddles, nurturing, and skin-to-skin contact. The down side . . . ? Well, my arms ache to wrap themselves protectively around my baby all night but my little star fish no longer needs them . . .

Chapter 8

Creating Confident Children

There are only two lasting bequests we can hope to give our children. One of these is roots, the other, wings.

—Hodding Carter, journalist and politician

I am always amazed how many people seem to think that the best way for a baby to mature into a confident child and independent adult is by teaching them how to be on their own as early as possible. My grandmother frequently commented, "Well he's got to learn he can't be with you all of the time," and it made me wonder exactly what it is that we think babies should learn. What do we teach them when we encourage their independence through controlled crying, by not letting them "manipulate" us into always holding them, or God forbid sleeping in a bed with them? What is the real message behind our actions? Do we teach them "it's good to be on your own, you will enjoy it" or do we create an even stronger need in them? Do we create a need to attach more, a need to cling to us when they can because they don't know when they will next be allowed to be so close to us? What happens when that need to be with us goes unmet for a long period? Would you bother trying to hug your partner any more if he forever pushed you away or would you give up? Would your need for holding have left or would you be repressing it? And what effects do you think that may have upon your confidence? Would you begin to question why you were no longer lovable and lose faith in yourself? And how might that translate into your everyday life? Might it make it hard for you to trust new friends, to open up to them? I am theorizing wildly here, I admit, or am I?

Before Independence Comes Dependence

My fourth child, Violet, arrived nearly five years after my firstborn. The time in between had given me five years of confidence, five years of wisdom, and five long years of regret and mommy guilt. From day one of her arrival, born into my own hands in our own home, she slept in my arms. I gave her as much of me as she wanted; it was as if we had blended into one new being. I was a vital part of her, as vital as any limb or organ, and she I, the "mother–infant dyad," as experts refer to it. We were cocooned in a perfect bubble of oxytocin love; it was as if for a while the outside world didn't really exist on the same plane. It was the first time I had experienced such intense feelings of love as a new mother and it felt surreal, but oh so very wonderful.

That's not to say that I love Violet any more than my other children, because I can genuinely say I love every one of them equally; differently, yes, but equally. There was something different about Violet, though, something chemical, a connection that I had no idea existed as a mother before. Why had I not experienced it with my first three children? It is something I lament to this day and the only answer I can give is that this was the first time I had stopped worrying about "how to be a good mother" or what people thought of me. It was the first time I went with my gut and ignored everything and everybody else.

When Violet was three months old we had her christened. My aunt rocked her to sleep while I fed and watered our guests. I bumped into her, cradling my sleeping baby, at the bottom of the stairs, looking most perplexed. I asked what was wrong. "But where is her crib?" she asked me. I smiled. "She doesn't have one." "Where does she sleep then?" "With me." "Oh." The silence spoke volumes. I knew what it meant and it was not the first or the last time I had such discussions. Having such a close attachment to our infants is not the thing that's done in our society. Rather, it is firmly entrenched in the domain of the "weird hippy tree hugger'" or the "earth mothers," and is viewed as extreme parenting. It is most definitely not considered normal nor healthy for the child to be "smothered" so much by the mother; indeed many believe that the mother must have psychological problems and unmet needs herself, that she is transferring her emotional problems onto her baby. Why can't people who feel this way not open their minds a little more and consider for just one moment that the very reverse may be true?

Throughout her babyhood Violet slept in my arms. In the day she slept in a wrap sling on my chest and at night in my arms in my bed . . . and then it happened. One night, when she was a toddler, she was fidgeting so much I couldn't sleep. So I asked her to please keep still in our bed and suggested that if she didn't want to she could sleep in her own bed. She had always had a bedroom and a bed that until this point had remained un-slept in, save for the few nights when I had fallen into it exhausted, desperate for an unbroken night's sleep and left her in the capable hands of my husband. It was 1 AM. She got up and toddled across our hallway in the pitch black, alone, climbed into her bed, pulled up the duvet, and went to sleep. I was stunned. That was it then. I now had an extremely independent toddler who no longer needed me.

Our co-sleeping journey was over, and it had finished with a bittersweet ending of pride and letting go. Where was the rod I had made for my back by letting her manipulate me for all of those months? What about the nay-sayers who told me that once we brought her into our bed we would never be able to get her out? She gave me a gift in those days and nights of contact and love and I gave her one in return. The gift of true confidence and independence, because before independence there must always be dependence; for a child to detach from us and go into the world with confidence and trust we must first open our arms for them to attach to us before opening them again for them to leave. Attachment is the real key to confidence.

Attachment Theory

Depriving a baby of the love and contact they need in infancy alters the neuroplasticity of the brain, changing the wiring in the relationship part of the brain, which affects the individual's experience of relationships long into adulthood. Research[63,64,65,66,67,68,69] on the impact of early attachments confirms that warm, responsive caregiving is essential to healthy brain development and ironically it is those babies who are allowed to be strongly attached to their parents as a baby that can truly self-settle as older children and adults. Indeed, Professor Darcia Narvaez, a key researcher in this field, believes that "warm, responsive caregiving like this keeps the infant's brain calm in the years it is forming its personality and response to the world," and comments:[70]

> With neuroscience, we can confirm what our ancestors took for granted—that letting babies get distressed is a practice that can damage children and their relational capacities in many ways for the long term. We know now that leaving babies to cry is a good way to make a less intelligent, less healthy but more anxious, uncooperative and alienated person who can pass the same or worse traits on to the next generation . . . According to a behaviourist view completely ignorant of human development, the child "has to be taught to be independent." We can confirm now that forcing "independence" on a baby leads to greater dependence. Instead, giving babies what they need leads to greater independence later.

Attachment theory considers the long-term effects that the formation (or lack) of a secure attachment with a known caregiver (usually the mother and/or father) during babyhood will have upon a child's life and future relationships. Much work on attachment theory was carried out after the Second World War and involved studying the effects of the separation of so many parents and infants during the evacuation and also those babies who had been orphaned by the war.

The founding father of attachment theory is the English psychiatrist and psychoanalyst John Bowlby. Bowlby devoted most of his career to the study of attachment in infants and adults, and believed that attachment was an evolutionary survival strategy for protecting babies from predators, a theory still widely held today. In 1951, Bowlby wrote a publication for the World Health Organization (WHO) in which he stated "the infant and young child should experience a warm, intimate, and continuous relationship with his mother (or permanent mother substitute) in which both find satisfaction and enjoyment and that not to do so may have significant and irreversible mental health consequences." Bowlby's work had positive effects on the care of children in institutions and care homes at the time and also greatly improved visiting access to children in hospital by parents.

Bowlby's work was revolutionary and paved the way for new thinking in child psychology. His work still has a major impact today. Bowlby's main idea was that a baby has a need for a secure relationship with his adult caregiver, and if this secure attachment, or bond, is not allowed to develop, normal social and emotional development would not occur. Once the baby has been allowed to form this secure attachment at a young age as he grows into toddlerdom and beyond, he uses his attachment figure as a "secure base" from which to explore the world around him.

Also, Bowlby believed that the process was not gender specific and that babies can and do form attachments to any consistent caregiver who is sensitive and responsive to their needs. Attachment theory states that an abrupt separation of the baby from familiar people or a lack of sensitive response from his parents can lead to short-term and possibly long-term negative impacts on the child's emotional life: "It is this complex, rich and rewarding relationship with the mother in the early years, varied in countless ways by relations with the father and with siblings, that child psychiatrists and many others now believe to underlie the development of character and mental health." How can it be that, despite Bowlby and those who have followed his path, we have known this for over sixty years, yet still persist in trying to train babies to become independent by enforcing separation from their parents?

The point I find so interesting and yet in many ways so sad when thinking about Bowlby's work was his belief that society should take a larger role in the raising of children and in particular in supporting the family, saying that "if a community values its children it must cherish its parents." He particularly believed that parents of children under the age of three should be supported to care for the child at home.

Is a Clingy Baby Really So Bad After All?

With all of this in mind why do we still refer to babies as clingy? Why do we praise the independence of a young baby so much? Why do we work so hard to keep babies in their own room, in their own beds, and away from us for almost half of a twenty-four-hour period almost as soon as they are born?

It is normal and healthy for our babies to "cling," or in the words of Bowlby: "Thus, just as animals of many species, including man, are disposed to respond with fear to sudden movement or a marked change in level of sound or light because to do so has a survival value, so are many species, including man, disposed to respond to separation from a potentially caregiving figure and for the same reasons." Sadly today these totally normal, healthy, and desirable responses in a baby so often lead to them being labeled as "needy" and "fussy" and the like, yet it is this response that allows the baby to develop true independence as they grow. Indeed the clingy, needy, fussy babies are perhaps the most desirable type. Now there's a thought!

What is even more sad is the fact we as a society ignore, or perhaps aren't even aware of to begin with, the mounting pile of evidence that quite clearly shows us a child who has not been allowed to be sufficiently attached during his babyhood is more likely to suffer from anxiety, depression, shyness, and commitment issues in adult relationships. I believe that the sooner society gets over this incorrect assumption the better, for maybe then we will stop advising mothers to "put that poor baby down, you don't want to make a rod for your own back" and begin to encourage them to go with their instincts and congratulate them for holding their babies. As psychologist Jeffry A. Simpson[71] says:

> Your interpersonal experiences with your mother during the first 12 to 18 months of life predict your behavior in romantic relationships 20 years later . . . Before you can remember, before you have language to describe it, and in ways you aren't aware of, implicit attitudes get encoded into the mind, about how you'll be treated or how worthy you are of love and affection. While those attitudes can change with new relationships, introspection, and therapy, in times of stress old patterns often reassert themselves. The mistreated infant becomes the defensive arguer; the baby whose mom was attentive and supportive works through problems, secure in the goodwill of the other person.

The Lasting Consequences of Forcing Independence

I can quite often spot a child who hasn't been allowed to attach fully to its parents, particularly the mother, as a baby, for they are often the ones who tend to be clingiest as a toddler, preschooler, or new school starter. They tend to be the ones who don't want their mommy to leave, begging her to stay, with big, fat tears rolling down their cheeks. In a quest to help, the nursery or school workers literally peel the sobbing child off the mother, despite the child's protests, and take them inside. Often you can still hear sobs five minutes later. Why would the children cry so much and need their mother so much? Is it because deep down something inside them is scared she won't come back?

If you listen to your instincts and stay close to your baby when they are young, the chances are you will forge a great bond of trust with them, which means that when they are ready to leave you they will never look back. I mean this literally. I am no longer allowed into the school grounds in the morning with Violet, now aged four, and she insists on me letting her walk from the car into the school playground and into her classroom by herself. I am relegated to the railings that I stand by each morning, watching my confident little girl go into the world on her own without so much as a second glance.

Another important point to consider is when is the right time to let go. When it is right for the child or for the parent? Or both? Is that possible? Is there a synchronicity in need of attachment and detachment? Can you ever be "too attached" to your child? Being truly baby and child led means we must follow their needs for independence as well as dependence. Or, as the great quote with which I opened this chapter says, "There are only two lasting bequests we can hope to give our children. One of these is roots, the other, wings." It is very hard, though, for just as we begin to find our place in life, so it changes again; it is so much easier to grow roots than to give wings.

Rosie's Story

When I decided to have a baby I was ready. I knew I wanted to spend a few years enjoying mothering, so we didn't mortgage ourselves up to the hilt, and we stayed in our small cottage. I felt that my career could wait. I had traveled and partied enough to not miss it for a few years, so I entirely felt committed to motherhood and happy to embrace every minute with my new baby.

I had read two books, one, sadly out of print, by psychologist Penelope Leach, entitled *The First Six Months: getting together with your baby*—a wonderful, confidence-boosting essay on what I suppose could now be loosely thought of as "attachment parenting." The other was *Three in a Bed* by Deborah Jackson. Both totally resonated with my feelings about mothering, so from that moment on I just followed my instincts—and my baby.

I always felt I instinctively knew—or could quickly determine—what he needed and what he didn't need. There was nothing I would rather have been doing than holding and gazing at my beautiful little boy. And that's how we spent our early days together: delighting in each other. Some years on and it's easy to recreate that emotional time, remembering how wonderful life was, just him and me—and husband of course.

As we were physically close, he hardly cried, because I just learned to understand what he wanted. Before I learned what he wanted, it seemed a pretty simple list of options to work through: hungry, thirsty, pooey, bored, tired.

There was also no question about him not sleeping with me or by my bed. Breastfeeding was easy at night, knowing that he would feed and sleep and I would sleep well too. We provided for each other exactly what we both needed. What could be lovelier than my little baby's skin next to mine: the feel of him; the smell of him; warm and cozy in bed together? It felt beautiful.

I trusted my instincts, and seeing that my baby was flourishing, my confidence grew. This is not to say that there weren't tears! There were many. Tears of frustration: will I ever get out of the house? And feeling very sorry for myself following mastitis and breast abscess, but they weren't tears about me and my baby.

I felt as if we were in our own little bubble. As long as we were happy, the world could wait. And it did. And when we were ready to step out into it, baby came too. He slept in our arms when he wanted, or in a Moses basket under a restaurant table, and he fed or had a drink when he wanted. He came on planes, trains, and in automobiles with us. He fitted into our family life—relaxed, sociable, and close. He was happy, so I was happy.

Everyone commented, "He's such an easy baby" and I thought, yes, he's easy because his needs are met. It seemed so obvious to me. When our baby's needs are met they can relax.

And so it continued . . . until we were eventually comfortable to be apart. From one morning a week at playgroup to starting school, he has always remained happy and contented. In the meantime, baby boy number two was born and I repeated my recipe for happy, confident children.

I have noticed over the years how comfortable they both are in their own skin. How comfortable they are with other people. Both were happy to travel independently at an early age and are now busy planning their own adventures in the world. I am regularly reminded of the phrase "before independence comes dependence." I was happy for them to be dependent. I embraced it.

I can see this may appear as if my memory has added a warm glow to the past, but I can honestly say it was the happiest time of my life, enabling my darling little boys to grow happily, healthily, and with confidence.

Chapter 9

Feeding Your Baby

Before I got married I had six theories about bringing up children; now I have six children, and no theories.

—John Wilmot, poet

One of the questions I am asked most commonly in my BabyCalm™ classes is, "Should he be on a feeding routine by now?" closely followed by "I'm worried about his feeding, particularly at night; my friend said he should only be feeding every three to four hours but he often feeds much more than that." Indeed many "baby experts" believe that babies who "snack" (as they call it) throughout the day will grow up to have weight problems as adults and that this snacking behavior is something to be stopped as soon as possible, in order that the baby doesn't manipulate you or grow up with unhealthy attitudes to food such as comfort eating. For the last fifty plus years there has been a growing trend of feeding by routine; that is only feeding your baby at times pre-determined by you, or the "baby expert," in order to get them "sleeping through the night" as soon as possible so that you may resume your normal life again.

Routine or Baby Led?

Many of the baby experts claim that establishing a feeding (and sleeping) routine as soon as possible after birth helps the mother to become confident in her new role. They often suggest that mothers who have no structure to their day (i.e,. those who rely on their baby to tell them when they are hungry, thirsty, and tired) are more likely to suffer from depression and anxiety. I often find completely the opposite to be true, for in my experience new moms frequently find these routines complicated, confusing, and tiring. They feel that they are tied to the house or unable to go out for the day because of their baby's schedule, rather like this new mom:

> In the early days I remember working hard to stick to the feeding routines, including pumping [breast milk] in the morning. It was hard work and I constantly felt I wasn't getting it right. When I finally "gave up" and moved to baby led feeding we were both almost instantly calmer and happier.

This comment from a BabyCalm™ teacher, who is a mom of five, particularly made me chuckle and nod in frantic agreement:

> I never tried a routine with any of my five. I am just not a "routine" person . . . and that is actually considered a failing in lots of spheres in life, I find. With babycare though it felt right . . . and in my honest opinion is the only way. My main problem was that I had to weather comments from my mother along the lines of "making a rod for your own back," etc. . . . so I really could have done with Baby-Calm™ back then to give me confidence.

Myth Versus Science

Some babycare experts say that if you space your baby's feeds three to four hours apart he will build a good appetite and will therefore "fill up" at the next feed, meaning he will be more contented and likely to sleep for longer periods, particularly at night. I would like to examine this assertion in the rest of this chapter, by looking at the science and the evidence, but first I would like to ask you to consider a few questions.

How do you decide when to eat and drink? Why did you last eat? Why did you have your last drink? Why do you sometimes not feel the need to snack between meals when at other times you feel like snacking constantly? Have you ever had days when you've been really thirsty, perhaps on a hot summer's day? Have you ever had bad PMS, or felt really sad, and really wanted to eat your way through the box of chocolates you bought as a gift for somebody but haven't yet given? I'm sure you can see what I'm getting at. Just as our appetite, thirst, and need for comfort changes each day so does that of your baby. Just as we don't always want to eat exactly the same amount at 8 AM, 1PM, and 6 PM every day, neither does your baby want to eat exactly the same amount at only 7 AM, 11 AM, 3 PM, and 7 PM every day either. Why is this? Because just as each baby is different, each day for each baby is different and to presume otherwise is just plain ridiculous. The following quotes from two of the moms who came to my classes sum up the situation very well:

> I never watched the clock; I just fed when they showed signs of being hungry. I never wait for a set time to eat; I just eat when I'm hungry, so why shouldn't I allow my baby to do the same?

> Everyone had so much advice about feeding my newborn, it was all so confusing, so I decided to forget everything I had read or been told, and just listen to my baby. And when I did that I found feeding so much easier and of course my baby was so much happier!

Cue Feeding

So when should you feed your baby? The simple answer is "When you think your baby needs feedin'." There is no magic formula, no timetables that need to be followed; you know your baby better than anyone else, so if you think he's hungry then he probably is and when it feels the right time to feed, it probably is. Your baby will show you cues, as this new mother's baby did:

> My wonderful husband quickly noticed our baby's early feeding cue was sniffing, and it helped so much! He never got to the point of crying if he was hungry, as I was aware of how he was letting me know before it got to that point. It made it easy to go with the flow and I was confident that I knew what he wanted.

Sometimes you might find you know your baby needs feeding even before he shows you, whether it is an inkling, a thought of "hmmm, he hasn't fed for a while, it must be time now," or in the case of this mom a more physical pointer:

> I just couldn't imagine not responding to my baby's needs—why wouldn't you? Feeding was always such a mutually satisfying experience; my breasts knew when it was time for a feed as much as my baby! It was such a bonding thing to be a part of.

This advice from the American Academy of Pediatrics gets it spot on: "Newborns should be nursed when they show signs of hunger, like being more alert or active, mouthing, or rooting. By the time a baby is crying from hunger, they have already been hungry for a while. In the early weeks, newborns should nurse about 8–12 times every 24 hours."[72] If you are breastfeeding, the World Health Organization (WHO) says, "Breastfeeding should be 'on demand,' as often as the child wants, day and night."

How to Know When Your Baby Wants a Feed

We have already seen that crying is a late indicator of hunger in a baby, and that before a baby cries to be fed he will already have shown you, in lots of little ways, some subtle, some less so, that he wants milk. Early hunger signs in babies usually include opening and closing the mouth, sucking the lips or hands, rooting on your chest, and fidgeting and squirming; it is only when these cues are missed that they will escalate into crying. This point is made by the American Academy of Pediatrics who say, "Your baby lets you know when he's hungry. Whenever possible, use the baby's signals rather than the clock to decide when to nurse him. . . . Your baby's feeding needs are unique. No book can tell you precisely how much or how often he needs to be fed, or exactly how you should handle him during feedings. You will discover these things for yourself as you and your baby get to know each other."

The key here is to watch your baby and not the clock! If you ignore the clock you allow your baby to control his own milk intake and listen to his body's signals, for both hunger and fullness, which will stand him in good stead for later in life, when as an adult he is more able to listen to his body and thus not under- or overeat.

Some mothers ask me if it is possible to demand feed if they are returning to work, to which I always reply "of course." Just because you are not with your baby it doesn't mean that your child's caregiver can't watch for his hunger cues and just because your baby is looked after by a nursery worker, relative, or babysitter it doesn't mean that he must automatically be fed to a routine.

Always remember you are the one who makes the decisions regarding your child's care, so you should be the one to decide how and when he is fed. It is pretty easy to teach your child's hunger cues to their new caregiver; you will only need to write them a short note and spend a few minutes discussing them in person before your first day back at work.

Length of Feeds

How long should you feed your baby for? Again the answer is simple—for as long as he wants! He'll let you know if he's starving and wants a big feed, or if he just wants a quick drink or snack, or a little comforting. Some babies are quick feeders, some take longer, whether they are breast or bottle feeding, and there is no set rule for the amount of time a feed should take, just as there is no set rule for how often a baby should feed and precisely the amount of milk they should consume per day.

Very often breastfeeding mothers can be more anxious than bottle feeding mothers about how much milk their baby is consuming. After all you can easily see exactly how much your baby has, or hasn't, drunk if you are feeding them with bottles, which is not the case with breasts. I will discuss the science of breastfeeding and milk production later in this chapter, but for now my answer to "How do I know he's getting enough milk?" is first a very simple "What goes in must come out" rule, and second, if he is growing and thriving (and gaining weight if you have your baby weighed), then he is getting enough. On the "what goes in must come out" front you are looking for roughly four to six wet diapers and three to four pooey diapers in every twenty-four hours when your baby is a newborn.

If you are bottle feeding your baby please skip over the next few paragraphs, which are specifically about breastfeeding, to Lisa's story at the end of this chapter.

Breastfeeding

In my work with very new mothers who are breastfeeding I find the same worries cropping up again and again: "I don't think I make enough milk, he's always hungry" and, "I'm tempted to give him a bottle in the evenings; I'm obviously not making enough as he feeds pretty much constantly between 7 PM and midnight." The most important point to make here is that both of those scenarios are totally normal and most definitely not a sign that the mom is incapable of providing all of the milk her baby needs. I would therefore like first to look at how breastfeeding works and second at the concept of "cluster feeding."

The easiest way I have found to reassure new moms that they have enough milk for their baby is to explain a little bit about the workings of breastfeeding. A basic understanding of lactation should be studied at school, along with the circulatory, gastrointestinal, and reproductive systems. I believe that the best way to increase breastfeeding rates is not to sensationalize it, but rather to normalize it, starting from a young age with removing toy feeding bottles from toy shops and teaching schoolchildren that breastfeeding is normal and natural.

So How Does Breastfeeding Work?

In the very early days of feeding your baby, your milk supply is controlled by hormones or "the endocrine control system." What does this mean for you? Put simply it means that for the vast majority of women making milk is something that just happens without any conscious input. In fact you were already making milk while you were pregnant, but you didn't notice because of hormones in your body (progesterone) suppressing the milk. After your baby was born progesterone levels in your body dropped dramatically, largely after your placenta was delivered, while levels of another hormone, prolactin, rose sharply just after the birth. These hormonal changes leave your body free to start secreting the milk it has been busy making for the last twenty weeks of your pregnancy.

Lots of people talk about their "milk coming in" after the birth, but what is actually happening is this change in hormone levels (namely progesterone and prolactin) allowing your body to secrete larger amounts of milk, the milk that you had already been making for so long, so actually rather than "coming in," your body actually starts "letting it out." This process is hormonally driven, which means that it is not dependent on your baby feeding, and indeed even if you bottle fed your baby from birth you would still produce milk at first.

After the first few days, milk production slowly shifts to an "autocrine control system," which means that it begins to be controlled by what is happening outside your body, i.e., your baby feeding. When your baby feeds and drains your breasts of milk this acts as a cue for your body to make more. When your breasts are full of milk they contain a protein called FIL (feedback inhibitor of lactation). This protein acts as an interpreter to tell your breasts to slow down their milk production; thus when your breasts are full, FIL slows down the synthesis of breast milk. When the breast is emptier, levels of FIL drop and so your body makes more milk again. What a wonderfully clever, but simple process and one that's so important to understand.

The key message to remember here is the more feeding you do the more milk you make, while the less you feed, and the longer spaced the feedings, the less you make. As Nancy Mohrbacher, author of the La Leche League International's *Breastfeeding Answer Book*, says, "Limited feedings by following a schedule during this critical time can limit or reduce a mother's milk supply. . . . Also, babies are not normally comfortable feeding at set intervals during their first six weeks, because their stomachs are so small."

With this in mind how do you think a routine of three- to four-hourly feeds can impact on milk supply when compared to the more normal "snacking" of a newborn who likes to be at the breast every hour or two? Which way of feeding is most likely to result in problems with milk supply? It's pretty clear. Nature intended babies to be at the breast frequently, so when we respond to our babies and allow them this frequent access in the early days we dramatically diminish the chance of having supply problems later on. If we put our young baby on a routine of enforced feeding times several hours apart we begin to create problems. It is little surprise that many of the mothers I have met who have followed these routines have had to move to bottle feeding sooner than they would like as they "ran out of milk."

I should add a quick note here, too, on expressing and pumping milk. If you don't know much about the mechanics of how a baby feeds it would seem simple to presume that if you pump milk regularly it doesn't matter if your baby feeds infrequently on a routine. Indeed, a "baby expert," aiming to get babies onto a routine and sleeping through as early as possible, might be tempted to advise new mothers to do this very thing, i.e., feed three to four hourly and pump milk to keep your supply up. This presumes that pumping works in the same way as a baby at stimulating milk supply and emptying the breast, but unfortunately it doesn't. Breast pumps are nowhere near as efficient at emptying milk as babies are and therefore nowhere near as efficient at increasing supply. Remember that the really simple solution to making more milk is to feed more, which is something this mom found out with her second baby:

> With my first baby I expressed and I never produced enough milk, probably because I was so anxious about it all. The second time around I just embraced the feeding, sat on the sofa and claimed the remote, and asked my husband to bring me water, water, and more water and lots of chocolate. I reminded my husband that looking after me was easier than constantly washing and sterilizing bottles.

I love how this new mother's father commented on his new grandson's lack of crying, which the mother puts down to listening to her baby's feeding cues:

> My parents visited us from overseas when my son was a month old. My dad was amazed that he didn't hear the baby's cries overnight, as that was obviously what he expected. But with my son close to me, feeding was easy, which meant I could feed and settle him before he became really upset.

Cluster Feeding (or "Will I Ever Get My Evenings Back?")

Lots of moms are particularly shocked to find that their baby wants to feed almost constantly all evening, particularly if they are happy to go a couple of hours between feeds in the day. It seems we have been brought up to believe that babies feed every three or four hours and we will know when they want feeding because they will cry lustily, so we tend to think that there is something terribly wrong when our newborn cries inconsolably unless he is on the breast for four hours solid every night. Most commonly the mother begins to worry that either there is a problem with her milk supply (that she is not making enough) or that there is something wrong with her baby.

In reality there is absolutely nothing wrong with the mom or the baby. This type of frequent feeding, also known as "cluster feeding," is totally normal and very, very common. It absolutely does not indicate problematic milk supply or a need to supplement with formula; as we now know the best way to increase milk supply is to feed, feed, and feed!

Cluster feeding can still come as a horrible shock though, particularly if you have been trying to put your baby on a routine of three- to four-hourly feeds with their last feed at 7 PM! Nancy Mohrbacher comments on cluster feeding saying, "New mothers who are unaware that this is normal often wrongly assume that they don't have enough milk. . . . What's important during this period is not that babies go two to three hours between feedings, but that babies get the right number of feedings overall."

Cluster feeding can be draining, but it is so often made worse by bad advice, as these moms found:

> My babies were all very heavy constant and cluster feeders. With my first I worried and struggled with the bad advice and support. I felt exhausted and drained but determined. In the end I did have some great support and realized I had to give myself to it for it to give to me in return, if you know what I mean?

> I freaked out about the hour-long plus evening feeding sessions and after pressure from my mother-in-law gave in and gave my baby a bottle of formula milk. It wasn't until my health visitor said it was totally normal that I accepted it and embraced the notion of being a feeding machine.

So what can you do if you have a cluster-feeding baby? The short answer is ride it out, remembering that letting your baby feed all he wants now will result in better milk supply and a happier baby in the long run. The long answer of course has to focus on you. Cluster feeding is absolutely exhausting; there's no getting away from it, particularly if you've spent a long day looking after your baby on your own and you are desperate for someone else to take the baby so you can have the evening to yourself and to rest. It is absolutely vital that here you put yourself first, in order to meet your baby's needs.

What does that mean? It means accepting any help that is offered and asking for any that is not. It means asking your partner, mom, sister, friend to cook for you, to bring you drinks, and to generally look after you. Your job is to nurture your baby and to put enough good food and drink into your body so that you can put milk into your baby's body in return. You need to eat, sleep, and rest, and then rest some more. Now is not the time to be worrying about housework or cooking; now is the time to look after yourself and remember how important you are. One day you'll look back on the traumatic memory of cluster feeding with pride at how you survived it, and so you should be proud; just like this mom below, you're doing an amazing job:

> When he put on weight I wanted to shout "I did that." I was so very proud that it was all my own work.

Lisa's Story

Feeding on demand wasn't really something I had thought about; it was just something that happened! My son, Bode, had jaundice after birth and everyone was very keen for me to feed him as much and as often as possible in order to resolve the jaundice.

It wasn't until about six weeks in that people began to mention that I needed to stop feeding him constantly and commenting on how he would sleep better if I got him into a routine. I was bombarded with information about how feeding and routine would help him to sleep better and how I should be keeping notes about which side he'd fed on and for how long. I found it all a bit overwhelming and quite stressful. I was also told to wake him at night and to feed him to get him to sleep better at night.

I did try waking him at night to feed and even tried taking notes for about a week and it left me exhausted and very stressed. Bode still woke every few hours and was not at all happy about being woken up to feed.

In the end I decided that routine feeding just wasn't working for us. I was much happier with the situation before and to be honest I worried he wasn't getting enough milk with the irregular feeding, so going back to feeding on demand seemed like the obvious solution to ease my worries.

The way I see it is if I'm thirsty or hungry I can get myself a drink or a snack, but as a baby Bode can't so why shouldn't I let him eat or drink when he wants to?

No, he doesn't sleep for twelve hours straight a night, but he is happy and that makes me happy and that is what truly matters. Bode is now twenty-three months old and still wakes occasionally, sometimes for a drink or a cuddle or just to tell me about the moon but he soon settles. We do have a routine I suppose, but it's our routine and I wouldn't have it any other way.

Chapter 10

When Something Is Wrong

The sound of a crying baby is just about the most disturbing, demanding, shattering noise we can hear. In the baby's crying there is no future or past only now. There is no appeasement, no negotiations possible, no reasonableness.

—Sheila Kitzinger, author of *The Crying Baby*

Sometimes, no matter what you do to calm them, some babies are still very unsettled; some may feed poorly, gain weight slowly, and sleep fitfully. This can be exhausting not only physically, but emotionally too. Not being able to calm and comfort your own baby can be one of the hardest feelings in the world, particularly if he seems to be in pain. All too often parents are dismissed by health professionals who tell them "he's fine—babies cry, that's just what they do" or suggest supplementing with formula if the mom breastfeeds or changing to "hungry baby" milk if she is bottle feeding. Many new moms can be left feeling helpless and don't know where to turn for help.

Sometimes, your baby's cries could be a sign of an underlying physical problem. There follows an explanation of some of the most common physical reasons why babies cry, although many of them, such as reflux and lactose intolerance, are still pretty rare and actually tend to be over-diagnosed. It's all too easy to self-diagnose, so if you think some of these descriptions do fit you and your baby please do consult a qualified professional.

Colic

Nobody really knows what colic is; it tends to be used as a catchall term to describe an unsettled crying baby, yet very often the label of "colic" is actually a sign of an undiagnosed problem such as tongue tie, breastfeeding latch problems, an over-stimulated baby, or a baby protesting at not being close enough to his parents. Colic in itself is not a disease or a disorder; it is really just an explanation of a baby who cries a lot. Diagnosing a baby with colic doesn't actually tell us what is wrong with the baby or help us to understand why the baby cries, and the cause often remains a mystery.

The official definition of colic is known as the Wessel Criteria, named after the American pediatrician of the same name. Wessel's definition[73] was based on observation with no scientific evidence behind it, yet the Wessel Criteria or the "Rule of 3s," that is a baby who cries for more than three hours a day, for more than three days a week, for over three weeks, is still commonly used by doctors around the world today. Wessel's definition of colic applies to around 25 percent of all babies, which to me is the first indication that there is another problem than just the tummy troubles usually believed to be the cause of colic at work. How can it be that 25 percent of all babies are so unsettled because of a tummy ache or trapped wind? Does it not seem strange to you that a quarter of all Western babies suffer from a severe tummy ache? What causes this mysterious tummy pain that is unique to small babies? Or perhaps the reason that they cry, the reason for their colic, is actually something totally unrelated to tummy problems and physical pain? This theory makes much more sense to me.

Our understanding of colic becomes even vaguer when we consider that it usually peaks between six to eight weeks of age and often resolves by twelve weeks for around 50 percent, with 90 percent resolved by nine months of age. By resolved, I mean that the babies stop crying so much. For most babies colicky crying is consigned to the evening, usually between what my husband and I used to call "the witching hours" of 6 to 9 PM, and I believe it is no small coincidence that this is usually the time when many babies cluster feed.

Colic is also reported more by mothers who have undergone a stressful pregnancy and have higher levels of stress and anxiety themselves.[74] Could it be that colic and crying in babies is in some way related to our levels of stress and anxiety as a mother? What is wrong with these babies? Signs of colic include prolonged crying, a baby drawing his legs into his body, his tummy going hard, and going red. There are signs we have already discussed earlier in the book that may not indicate tummy ache, trapped wind, or pain at all; in fact signs that for many babies show that they are simply unhappy.

Some evidence[75,76,77] suggests that limiting the mother's diet may improve colic symptoms if she is breastfeeding, with the main culprits usually being the cruciferous vegetables (such as cabbage, cauliflower, and broccoli), cow's milk, chocolate, onions, and caffeine.

There is no evidence for anything more than a placebo effect for many over-the-counter colic remedies. Worryingly, the two main colic remedies available, containing simethicone (used to release gas bubbles in the tummy) and lactase enzymes (to break down lactose in babies believed to have a lactose intolerance), have not been shown to have any consistent effect on infantile colic in scientific research.[78] This is particularly alarming when you consider that research suggests around three-quarters of babies today are exposed to some form of medicinal product before eight weeks of age.[79] Similarly, switching to soy-based formula has not been shown to have any determinable effect on colic symptoms.[80]

How best to deal with colic then? If a mom in my BabyCalm™ classes confides in me that she is concerned her baby has colic I usually suggest all of the calming techniques discussed throughout this book, combined with a visit to a cranial osteopath or chiropractor. If the mom in question is breastfeeding I always, without fail, suggest she seeks help from a breastfeeding counselor or lactation consultant, as for many breastfeeding moms the true cause of colic is actually an underlying breastfeeding problem.

Cranial Compression and Birth Trauma

If a baby is born by Caesarean, ventouse, or forceps my ears always prick up immediately, especially if the labor has been long and involved malpresentation (the baby lying in the wrong position). In my career I have worked very closely with a chiropractor who specializes in working with new babies and over the years of sharing clients I have learned very much from her.

I have already looked briefly at chiropractic and osteopathic care earlier in the book, because I believe it is very important in babycare. It may help you to understand this if you can imagine your head being crooked at an unusual angle for several weeks or even months, and then somebody pushes your head down into that position even harder for a good minute every three minutes for fourteen hours or even more. You would probably have a very bad headache and neck ache. I have seen many babies in obvious discomfort, several with torticollis (the medical term for stiff neck), unable to turn their heads. Aside from the discomfort this naturally causes, a baby with a stiff neck can also have problems feeding as it might be painful for them to turn their head to do so.

There is another area where chiropractic and osteopathy might be particularly helpful. During labor the baby's cranial bones move and overlap (think of the odd shape of your baby's head after birth); this molding is completely normal, as it helps your baby's head to become as small as possible so that it can fit through your pelvis, even if that's not the way he ultimately came out. The baby's cranial bones usually then return to their normal position over the first few days following birth, mostly via the process of the baby sucking (and the movement of the upper and lower jaw), which stimulates the base of the skull, via the palate.

What Happens During A Chiropractic Or Cranial Osteopathic Treatment?

Your first appointment will probably last for around 30 minutes. During that time the chiropractor or osteopath will ask you questions about your baby's behavior, feeding, and sleeping patterns, and will also ask you about your birth experience, including whether your baby was born by C-Section, ventouse, forceps, or an unassisted vaginal delivery. They will also be interested in the length of your labor and your baby's birth weight. All this information is very important as it tells them a little about any problems your baby may be experiencing.

After taking a short medical history for your baby the chiropractor or osteopath will gently feel your baby's skull, neck, and spine, and will often perform small manipulations to your baby's skull, neck, or spine, possibly performing some very light massage to certain areas of their body. You will be present at all times and will be able to comfort your baby if he cries and feed right away afterwards. Many babies find this examination and resulting treatment very calming and lots often have a long sleep afterwards.

After this examination the chiropractor or osteopath will be able to tell you if they think they have found any areas of concern and whether they think they can do anything to help. They should then discuss any treatment plan with you, including how many sessions they think your baby will need and the cost.

Sometimes, however, things don't return to normal and often abnormal skull compression becomes noticeable via the baby's feeding habits and need to suck much more than usual; sucking being the way your baby tries to resolve the problem himself. If the baby's vagus nerve (the nerve directly linked to digestion) is compressed, this can also have noticeable effects on a baby's digestive system, often causing him pain. All of this is more likely to happen if the labor is long, the baby is malpresented, or is born via emergency C-Section, forceps, or ventouse.

I asked a few mothers about their experiences of chiropractic and osteopathic treatment for their babies while researching this book:

I saw a chiropractor with both children as babies, having given birth to them both by C-Section. He explained that Caesarean births can mean that the cranium isn't moved as beneficially as with vaginal birth. It was a very gentle treatment, so much so that my baby slept through it! Neither of my babies suffered from colic or being unsettled and I do think chiropractic care helped.

During pregnancy I'd read about how cranial osteopathy could help soothe tension in babies so I decided to visit one with my newborn even though our birth was straightforward. We had one appointment and the osteopath was really genuine, saying that she had released some minor tummy tension and we wouldn't need another appointment. It gave me peace of mind that I was helping my baby to be as comfortable as possible.

Visiting a good chiropractor or cranial osteopath can make a profound difference for some new parents and babies. I am so passionate about its benefits—I believe it should be available free of charge to all new parents. After all, we check a baby's hips after birth, so why then would we not check his skull and spine?

Reflux

Many parents suspect their baby has reflux; they are often concerned that their baby is sick regularly (which is perfectly normal in young babies) and seems uncomfortable. Genuine reflux, however, is grossly over-diagnosed in babies. That's not to say the condition doesn't exist because it does and it can be very tough to live with, but I believe that far more babies than necessary are being prescribed reflux medications when perhaps another underlying issue is really at fault.

I estimate that around 10 to 20 percent of the babies who come to my BabyCalm™ classes are being given infant Gaviscon, but as with colic, can it really be that so many have a problem and that so many of our babies need medicating? Indeed, pediatric gastroenterologist Eric Hassall[81] comments, "These symptoms and signs are just 'life,' not a disease, and as such do not warrant drug therapy."

Ironically I tend to find it is those babies who really do have a problem that miss out on a diagnosis, particularly in the case of silent reflux.

So what is reflux? Reflux is what happens when the contents of a baby's stomach come back up into his esophagus and sometimes into his mouth, largely because the sphincter action of the baby's diaphragm isn't completely developed. As the sphincter action develops the reflux tends to decrease. This action is pretty common, though, with up to 50 percent of babies suffering from reflux; however it is only problematic for a tiny percentage. When it is problematic it can cause a large range of symptoms. Reflux can affect all babies, however they are fed.

Signs of Infant Reflux

- Excessive crying, particularly after a feed
- Arching back after a feed
- Excessive vomiting, often projectile
- A persistent night-time cough

- A persistently runny nose
- Very frequent waking during sleep
- Baby is happier when held in an upright position
- Acidic-smelling breath
- A hoarse cry, as if he has a sore throat
- Poor weight gain
- Excessive irritability
- Very frequent feeding

Silent reflux is used to describe the same condition, however in this case the most common symptom of projectile vomiting is missing and the baby may show no outward symptoms at all, hence the name "silent." Silent reflux can be very distressing as it often manifests as a very unhappy baby who wakes extremely frequently during the night and is very hard to settle. However, as the outward symptoms are not there it is often much harder to diagnose.

Tips to Cope with Reflux

- Try to keep your baby upright for at least thirty minutes after a feed. If your baby is formula fed you may have to hold him upright for longer as formula milk takes longer to digest than breast milk.
- Special sleep positioners and wedges can work well for babies with reflux; they help to keep your baby in a more upright position making him more comfortable during sleep. These can be found easily on the internet.
- Wearing a baby with reflux in a sling can be a life saver; not only does the sling hold him in an upright position, but the close proximity to you can help to calm him and alleviate any pain he may be feeling.
- Avoid putting tight clothing on your baby, particularly around his tummy, which may aggravate the problem. Loose fitting all-in-ones and onesies will probably be the most comfortable garments for him.

- If you are breastfeeding you can try to remove foods that aggravate your baby's reflux from your diet. Common culprits are dairy products, spicy food, caffeine, citrus fruits, and seeded fruit such as strawberries.
- Babies with reflux tend to respond well to more frequent, smaller feeds.
- Baby massage, particularly focusing on the tummy, can be very helpful for soothing babies with reflux.

Lactose Intolerance and Cow's Milk Protein Allergy

Many people use the terms lactose intolerance and milk allergy interchangeably, but they are actually very different conditions.

Cow's Milk Protein Allergy

About 2 percent of babies suffer with a cow's milk protein allergy (CMPA), though the incidence is lower in breastfed babies. Symptoms tend to appear very early, particularly when cow's milk is introduced to the baby's diet (which can happen indirectly through the mother's consumption if she is breastfeeding), although some can be late in onset. A milk protein allergy is very rare in exclusively breastfed babies. Reactions occur in the baby's body when their immune system mistakes milk protein for something foreign that the body should fight, triggering an allergic response. Nobody really knows why some babies suffer from CPMA, though the general belief is that the problem is genetic in origin. There is unfortunately no one definitive test to diagnose CPMA; usually a diagnosis is arrived at through a series of blood tests, skin prick tests, and stool testing.

The symptoms of cow's milk protein allergy are:

- diarrhea (which may contain blood)
- vomiting

- excessive irritability
- skin problems, such as eczema
- failure to thrive and slow weight gain.

The only treatment for CMPA is to avoid the source of the problem. Breastfeeding mothers are therefore advised to completely remove dairy from their diet and babies who are bottle fed will be prescribed special hypoallergenic formula milk. Most babies usually outgrow CMPA by the age of four.

Lactose Intolerance

Lactose intolerance is caused by the body's inability to digest lactose, a sugar found in milk. The intolerance is caused by a lack of the enzyme lactase in the baby's body. Lactase helps the body to digest the milk sugar lactose.

Symptoms of lactose intolerance include:

- diarrhea
- vomiting
- tummy pain
- excessive wind
- constipation.

Lactose intolerance is not dangerous, in that the body is not reacting in the same way as it does to a cow's milk protein allergy, but it can make babies very uncomfortable. Many babies who are lactose intolerant can tolerate yogurt, butter, and cheese, as they contain less lactose than milk itself.

My second baby suffered from lactose intolerance. He did not display any symptoms when he was exclusively breastfed; they only appeared when he was weaned and I gave him either cow's milk or formula. He seemed to change overnight from being a happy, relaxed baby to being bad tempered and sleepless. Looking back now it's clear that he was uncomfortable as he would suffer terribly from wind and constipation and his poor little tummy became very bloated. His skin became very dry, patchy, and spotty as opposed to the beautiful soft, clear skin he had when he was exclusively breastfed, and he developed a permanently runny nose and rattled cough. We switched him to special lactose-free milk and he improved greatly within a matter of days, but on days when he accidently consumed cow's milk we would all suffer for the next few days. He outgrew the problem by the time he went to school and now has no issues with milk.

Latch Problems in Breastfed Babies

If a breastfed baby is very unsettled the chances are the problems lie with the breastfeeding and specifically the latch. Even if you think your baby is latching on correctly it is *always* worth seeking advice, in person, from a breastfeeding counselor or a lactation consultant, as they can spot many problems that you may not be aware of yourself. As a general rule if feeding is hurting you, it is highly likely there is something wrong with your latch.

Despite popular advice breastfeeding is not meant to hurt. Bleeding and cracked nipples and mastitis are absolutely not normal and not just part and parcel of breastfeeding; they are a sign that something is not quite right. If your breastfed baby seems to be constantly hungry, even after a feed, or is not gaining weight well, the chances are there is something wrong with the latch, even if a medical professional has told you it looks fine. I cannot highlight enough here how important it is that you have a qualified professional watch you feed and check your baby's positioning, as getting help early can save so much trouble and heartache down the line, and in most cases positioning problems are very easy to rectify, leaving you to experience breastfeeding as the pain-free, enjoyable event it should be.

Some signs that a breastfed baby may not be positioned correctly:

- The baby is fussy and irritable.
- The baby has diarrhea or constipation.
- The baby makes clicking sounds while he feeds.
- Your baby's cheeks dimple when he feeds.
- Your baby's ears do not wiggle when he feeds.
- Your baby only takes your nipple and not the surrounding areola.
- Your nipples are sore, cracked, or bleeding.
- You develop mastitis, a blocked milk duct, or severe engorgement.
- Your baby's feeds are either very short or very long.
- Your baby does not seem satisfied after a feed.

Tongue Tie

It is estimated that up to 10 percent of newborn babies suffer from tongue tie, yet the vast majority of these go undiagnosed, which can cause weeks or months of misery for both parents and baby. This is especially frustrating as diagnosing and rectifying a tongue tie is relatively easy and the effects of releasing a tongue tie can dramatically improve many issues. Many of us are familiar with the term "tongue tied" only with relevance to speech problems and not being able to say what we want to say without getting in a muddle, yet so few are aware of the actual physical problem that can so commonly affect babies.

Tongue tie, or ankyloglossia, as it is known medically, is a birth defect in which the baby's frenulum, the piece of skin that loosely attaches the tongue to the base of the mouth, is unusually short. This has the result of holding the tongue down and often dramatically restricting the tongue's range of movement.

Not all tongue ties cause problems though. My first baby was born with a mild tongue tie, which caused no issues and had broken by itself by the time he was four months old. For those that are more severe, where the tongue is almost fused to the base of the mouth, problems can be dramatic. This mom describes what feeding an undiagnosed tongue tied baby felt like:

My baby fed on demand and took the colostrum frequently day and night. However, by the third day, my nipples had become extremely sore and cracked. I was unsuccessfully using two different creams, said to help heal and soothe nipples, frequently, but latching her on was becoming more and more painful. I tried different positions and used pillows to help with the angle, but I was tense and the toe-curling sensation at every feed was becoming difficult to bear . . .

My milk came in eight days after the birth and my breasts swelled from a C to an E cup. I invested in new bras and this eased some of the discomfort I had been feeling. My nipples, however, were increasingly sore and often bled in my baby's mouth. I would walk around the house without any top on, not able to let anything touch the skin, sometimes even just air was painful. I used Savoy cabbage leaves chilled in the fridge, gel breast pads, and silicone nipple shields . . . anything from the shops that claimed to help. The pain was still severe and it became evident that the cracked nipples had caused further issues. After each feed, I had a deep, uncomfortable sensation under my armpits. The doctor confirmed that I had thrush and an infected nipple. We both had to be treated. But the thrush was deep and it felt like it was getting worse. . . . Upset, frustrated, and my body in bits, I was very low at this point. It was only my determination that overcame the pain every time I fed—I could not even entertain giving up, not now I had gone this far, I wanted to succeed.

Problems potentially caused by tongue tie in young babies include the following:

- poor latch when breastfeeding
- bleeding and sore nipples when breastfeeding
- mastitis when breastfeeding
- problems with bottle feeding if the baby is unable to form a seal around the teat and cannot take milk from the bottle easily as a result
- babies can be frustrated when feeding
- baby's appetite often not satiated after a feed
- failure to thrive/poor weight gain
- windy and irritable babies.

If you think your baby may be tongue tied it would be a good idea to visit a breastfeeding counselor or International Board Certified Lactation Consultant (IBCLC) as soon as possible, even if you are not breastfeeding. They will be able to check for you and refer you to somebody who will be able to release your baby's tongue tie.

In babies a frenotomy, or tongue tie release (often scarily referred to as "snipping"), is a simple and quick procedure where the tie is carefully cut underneath the tongue. Sometimes there may be a small amount of bleeding, but babies can feed right away afterward and no special aftercare is needed. Parents often report seeing dramatic results immediately after the procedure, with babies feeding better almost right away and other problems diminishing quickly afterwards. The same mom above describes the procedure of having her baby's tongue tie released and how it helped:

> I went to a breastfeeding support group and the breast-feeding counselor there confirmed that my baby had a posterior tongue tie. This was the missing piece as to

why the latch was so difficult and why she hadn't been taking my milk as she should. The breastfeeding team put the ball in motion to get us referred in order to get this addressed as quickly as possible. Within a week the specialist midwife at the hospital called me to make an appointment. A week later my baby had her tongue tie cut. It was a simple procedure performed by the nurse. She did cry, but fed from me right afterwards. I was told that this was now make or break. She would either get the hang of the latch or not. She was five weeks old.

We persisted. About a week later, I became pain free. . . . We are a success story. Almost five months on and I am still exclusively breastfeeding. I am so happy that I persisted, but now have such a great insight into why women give up. It is hard and the support isn't always found in time.

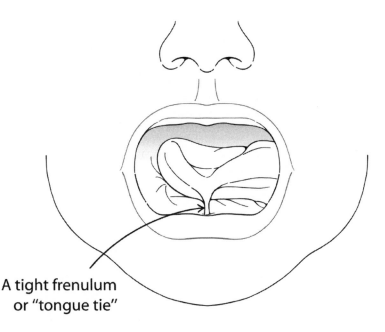

A tight frenulum or "tongue tie"

Lucy's Story

I found the first three days with Ed very difficult. For the first night he was like a dream baby. He fed, slept a few hours, fed again, and slept. I was amazed and thought I had given birth to a very, very easy baby. On the third night, though, I really started to struggle to feed him. He just wouldn't latch on. I phoned the ward in desperation in the middle of the night; they told me to express and cup or bottle feed. I had no idea what they meant by "cup feeding" so I gave him a bottle and he loved it, it was so easy for him. We then went really downhill, and he did not want to even try to latch on, but just wanted a bottle. With hindsight, it would have helped so much to have been shown how to cup feed him to get us through the tricky bit instead of giving him the bottle, which is where the real problems started.

He was always a bit of a wriggly feeder on my breast but we thought it was because of the problems we had getting started. However, it got worse and worse; he was also a very, very sicky baby. I was always covered in baby sick; I even stopped getting changed, as I just didn't have the time or the spare clothes. I never went anywhere without a raft of muslin squares covering me. He also slept very badly, waking frequently and being very fussy, he just wouldn't settle at night. Ed was finally diagnosed at four months with gastroesophageal reflux disease. At this age, he really took a turn for the worse. The dairy passing through my breast milk also caused problems, and I had to give up dairy and soya as well. Although I now think the issue of dairy and soya intolerance was separate to the reflux, there is no doubt that both of these things caused real problems over his first year.

He was prescribed very strong medication and the dose had to be increased a number of times. The consultant never really saw it as a significant problem as he always appeared healthy, gained weight, and hit all the developmental milestones. He truly was a delightful baby in all other aspects! As far as the consultant was concerned, the impact on the rest of the family was just insignificant. Even on the medication, he would generally go to bed quite happily but then have two periods of waking in the night (apart from for feeds). The first time, he would scream for up to two hours (sometimes even three), and then finally sleep before waking for the second bout of screaming, which would last for about the same time.

We always brought him into our bed, even though there was nothing that either of us could do to calm him; he was in so much pain. Every time, it broke my heart to hear him, but I couldn't even hold him as he writhed so much. He just wanted to lie flat and writhe around until it finally passed. We started to take it in turns to stay in bed with him while the other one went down to the spare room to try to get some sleep. We were exhausted every day. I really struggled when my husband worked away, as I didn't really have anyone who could come to stay to help me out. Some nights were so bad I just look back and marvel that I did cope. I'd seen my GP and he offered me drugs for depression. I was astounded. Yes, I sometimes felt that I was losing my mind, and I was weepy and confused, but I was suffering from severe sleep deprivation. Let's not forget, this technique is used as a means of torture in many arenas of war. I certainly never felt hopeless about the future; far from it, we lived on the assurance that "this, too, will pass," although we knew it could take a year.

We all learned a lot through this difficult year. I learned that I don't need as much sleep as I thought I did. I learned to appreciate all forms of rest, even if I wasn't asleep, but lying and allowing myself to relax was often enough to just recharge a little. I learned that no matter how annoyed I was at being kept awake, I was never angry with Ed, only heartbroken that he was suffering so much. I would have done anything to take his pain away. We learned that consultants' appointments for four minutes every three months are not enough for holistic understanding and treatment of a baby. We learned that a parent's common sense is far more valuable. I learned how love can hold everything together in the most difficult of circumstances, for everyone in the family.

Strangely, although 2011 is without a doubt one of the most difficult years I have ever experienced in my life, I still have many memories of love, laughter, and fun. Although Ed is still unable to tolerate dairy at the age of fourteen months, he has been sleeping without pain for over a month now. He now has soya in his diet and although it is hard to cater to, we have adapted and cope very well. I feel so much stronger and able to cope with pretty much anything that life throws at me because of this experience, and every day I feel blessed to have a wonderful, supportive husband and two delightful, healthy children.

Kate's Story

My baby, Louis, and I had a very rocky start to life after a traumatic birth—a lengthy labor resulting in a C-Section. I really wanted to breastfeed; I always knew before I had Louis that I would try, but I believe that because I didn't get the birth I wanted this made me even more determined and I became pretty desperate for it to work out.

We needed help as Louis was a very unsettled baby; he didn't stop crying the first night we got home from hospital unless he was on my boob. . . . I now realize he was hungry. He was also losing weight (he had lost 13 percent of his birth weight by day five) and the advice of the midwives was to supplement with formula, something I didn't want to do. Nobody once looked in his mouth or listened to my complaints of sore nipples; they would just say, "That's just how it is, love." All in all it was a very stressful time. Luckily for us our amazing doula put us in touch with a fabulous International Board Certified Lactation Consultant who visited us and observed feeds before giving us a plan of action. Afterwards things seemed to be going well, however Louis then stopped gaining weight once again and became very windy.

After her second visit the lactation consultant confirmed that Louis was showing lots of signs of being tongue tied. She explained that although he was feeding and gaining weight very slowly his short frenulum prohibited his tongue from transferring milk to his body properly and as a result he couldn't get to the rich fatty milk. Once diagnosed our lactation consultant arranged for Louis to have his tongue tie snipped very quickly and effectively. Since then we have never looked back!

I spent a lot of time at home during the first six weeks of Louis's life determined to get the feeding right and expressing to top him up as he couldn't feed effectively. During that time our lactation consultant was always on hand with information and knowledge to ensure we knew Louis had started feeding correctly, from emailing clips of effective milk transfer, to recommending books for me to read and giving me the confidence to believe in my maternal instincts.

Now, ten months on and we are still breastfeeding, which feels amazing. It has been a rocky road but luckily we have had the support of some fantastic people along the way.

I had never even heard of tongue tie, but the symptoms are quite obvious so at least we will know what to look out for next time!

Chapter 11

Birth Trauma
and Bonding

*It seems that many health professionals involved in antenatal
care have not realized that one of their roles should be to
protect the emotional state of pregnant women.*

—Dr. Michel Odent, obstetrician and author

Whenever I meet a new mom for the first time at a BabyCalm™ workshop or class I always start with the same question: "So, tell me about your birth."

Mostly it's met with confusion, wrinkled eyebrows, and exchanged curious looks, and very often they ask me, "Why?" right back. After all they haven't come to see me to talk about their birth experience; they have come to see me to work out why their baby cries so much and to get help in calming him down and getting a little more sleep at night. To me, however, your postnatal experience and birth are so inextricably linked it is absolutely impossible to understand any issues parents are having with their newborn baby unless we go right back to the beginning (sometimes the cause goes even farther back, to pregnancy and before—I'm very aware of that too). For as long as I work with new parents I will always ask that question and I truly believe that anybody working with new parents must begin with considering the baby's birth and how the experience has affected all involved in order to begin to really help.

The Lasting Physical Consequences of Birth for the Mother

I felt like I had been involved in a full-on boxing match after giving birth to my babies, even those where the birth was easy and gentle. I ached in muscles I didn't even know I had; sitting down was nigh on impossible for most of the first week; and my stomach felt as if the muscles had given up. I was too scared to poo in case I split my stitches, despite being given copious amounts of stool softeners and laxatives and taking a jug of warm water into the bathroom with me. I'd never seen so much blood in my life and the after-pains were severe, particularly with my third baby. I had given birth to an 11-pound (5-kilogram) baby at home in water with not even a whiff of gas and air, but after his birth I was begging anybody who would listen for drugs. I didn't care what the drugs were, the stronger the better, just something, anything, to take away the awful excruciating after-pains. I remember the first night after he was born sitting on the sofa at 2 AM, feeding him and sobbing loudly, tears rolling down my face with the terrible after-pains. All of this was after natural births too; moms whose babies are born by C-Section have my utmost respect, as becoming a mother while recovering from major abdominal surgery is never the easy option, whatever the press might say about being "too posh to push."

I have met too many women suffering with perineal trauma, poorly stitched episiotomies, and the like, which not only cause great physical discomfort, but emotional too—which naturally has a knock-on effect long after the event. We don't seem to talk about moms physically healing after the birth though, and it's certainly not something I remember covering in antenatal classes. However, the physical scars of birth can be long lasting and so very damaging, even long after they have healed.

Suggestions for Post-Birth Physical Healing

When a new mom asks me for my top "post-birth" recovering tips these are usually what I recommend:

- Lavender oil in a bath. Add six to eight drops into a saucer of milk, swish with your finger, and then pour into a freshly run warm bath. The milk may seem a little strange, but it acts to disperse the oil, otherwise it would sit in big blobs on top of the water. Lavender is wonderfully soothing for new mothers; it is also naturally antiseptic.
- Calendula tincture, six drops diluted in half a cup of lukewarm water, and used as a wash on stitches.
- Don't be too ashamed to wee in the bath or the shower! This might sound horrible, but for the first few times after birth, particularly if you have had stitches, you might find you are a lot more comfortable standing in the shower or sitting in a bath of warm water when you need to wee.
- Big panties—the bigger the better. Waist-high ones are great if you have had a C-Section; don't waste your money on special post C-Section panties and definitely don't buy poor-quality, uncomfortable-feeling disposable panties, but instead buy a batch of extra-large sized, high-waisted, cotton panties from a cheap store or supermarket.
- Forget maternity pads. They tend to be big and bulky yet not particularly absorbent and also have an irritating habit of falling out of your panties and sticking to the inside of your leg. I found, entirely accidentally, that opening out a newborn diaper and placing it inside your panties works infinitely better than a maternity pad; it doesn't come loose, is softer on your stitches, and is thinner yet much more absorbent.

- Peppermint tea is very helpful if you have had a C-Section, to remove the trapped air bubbles that can cause horrible chest and shoulder pain.
- Don't get dressed! I have often found that if a new mom lounges around in pajamas and a robe, people look after her, whereas the minute she gets dressed or puts on make-up people seem to think she is back to normal and tend to help less.
- Enjoy your babymoon. Don't rush off out, take it easy, and rest. It's quite common to bleed more heavily after the birth if you have overdone it in the early days. Enjoy these precious moments with your newborn and don't be in a rush to return to normal life too quickly. Keep visitors to a minimum; never be afraid to say "not today, thank you, I'm very tired." Ask anybody who does visit to come armed with dinner or lunch for you too.

In my ideal world all new mothers would also be visited by a chiropractor or osteopath shortly after the birth. Having suffered from hideous symphysis pubis disorder (SPD, now known as pelvic girdle pain, or PGP) during my first two pregnancies I was amazed to find with my third baby that pregnancy didn't have to hurt!

The Lasting Psychological Consequences of Birth for the Mother

When he was born, I lifted him up through the water and snuggled him to my chest. It was like the world had stopped; everything went quiet and this wave of purity washed over me. I was hooked. I was euphoric. I was in love.

Was that how it was for you? So often I work with new mothers ashamed to admit that they still don't know if they really love their babies, or that it took a long time for that love to grow, quietly confessing that for them there was no instant "rush of love." Sadly I hear these sorts of comments much more frequently than the quote above. These are just some of the recollections of moms I have worked with:

> I had a C-Section under general anesthetic. I woke up totally detached. I saw my husband holding a fully dressed bundle and my first thought was, "Where did he get this child from—has he given away my newborn?"

> I felt disappointed and sad.

> I had a shocking first birth which left me disconnected from my body, in shock, and exhausted. I was glad the baby was OK, but I was so disappointed in myself for letting them do all the things to us that they did. I felt that we were lucky to be alive and that we had endured the birth rather than exalted in it. I definitely would never wish the experience on my worst enemy. My son still has a scar on his head from the ventouse pull. I will always feel bad about that for him, let alone the scars I was left with.

> I felt like I had had a butchering, not a birth. It was an awful experience and it took me two years to be able to talk about it without crying! My body has still not recovered properly. I was so ill I had no interest in my baby for forty-eight hours. The midwives took him away to feed as I was incapable of doing anything. I blame it all on being induced.

Dr. Michel Odent, the renowned French obstetrician and author, says, "We now have scientific evidence that explains how the capacity to love develops through a complex interaction of hormones, hormones that are secreted during many experiences of love and close human interaction including sexual intercourse and conception, birth, lactation, and even sharing a meal with loved ones. The role of oxytocin, the 'love hormone,' is particularly important. Natural oxytocin delivered by human touch, but not synthetic oxytocin delivered by an intravenous drip, has important effects on many organs in the body, including the brain."

We know that the blood–brain barrier prevents artificial oxytocin from entering the brain. This may not seem important when you are told that you need an oxytocin drip to "speed up" or even start your labor, or when you are told it's best you have an injection to deliver your placenta and prevent blood loss (all of which contain synthesized oxytocin), but when you understand that this results in a direct lack of oxytocin circulating the maternal brain we begin to realize quite what catastrophic effects the use of these supposedly "safe" chemicals can have upon the bonding of mother and child. We know oxytocin is the hormone of love and if we are depriving mothers of this in their brain perhaps we should be concerned about how we may be damaging the love process between mother and baby.

It is not just synthesized oxytocin that can impact on bonding; a lack of skin to skin after the birth, swaddling babies with hats on in cribs, and our obsession with getting babies dressed as quickly as possible in order to "warm them up" can have an impact on early bonding too, as can "waking" mothers in the first hour after birth, by switching on bright lights, talking to her, prodding and poking her, encouraging her to go to the toilet, or change position to deliver the placenta. These things can all impact bonding. In fact, humans are the only species who do not reject their young under these circumstances; all other primates reject their newborn offspring when placed in an artificial environment full of interference and lacking in oxytocin. Birth, and particularly the first hour after birth, is not meant to be like this. We are fighting a battle with bonding before we have even begun.

I have experienced birth and bonding both ways. My first two births were full of intervention. During the first one I had "failed to progress" and I was administered a drip to ramp up my contractions. My waters were roughly broken; I was subjected to six intrusive vaginal examinations and then given a time limit in which to produce a baby. I didn't care, though, as the only thing that mattered to me was ending the pain and the fear and I begged for an epidural. My baby was born and immediately taken away to be dried off and checked over while I was injected with syntometrine before I had a chance to say anything to deliver the placenta.

My second birth was an induction for pre-eclampsia and I was told that because I was ill, I had no choice but to have syntometrine to deliver the placenta, frequent vaginal examinations, constant monitoring, and a pediatrician to take away my baby at birth to "check him over," rather than the immediate skin to skin I had requested. In fact we had no skin-to-skin contact until we left the hospital three days later.

Did I fall instantly in love with those babies? No. My first I adored by about the age of three weeks; my second, well, if I'm honest it took years to feel that bond. I loved him, but we had to really work on getting that chemical bond to exist. This is really no surprise considering my induction, the fact that he was whisked away by pediatricians and given back to me fully swaddled, and that I was kept on the busy ward for observations for three days after the birth. Every time I brought him into my bed to sleep, desperate for some contact, I was told he was not allowed to sleep with me and on several occasions I even woke to find he had been taken from my arms and put back in the crib.

And then there were births number three and four. My third baby, Rafferty, arrived at home, in a birth pool, in my dimly lit living room with an incredibly respectful midwife who didn't touch us at all. Nobody, but my husband and me, laid hands on my baby until he was three days old. Now I knew what they meant by "love at first sight." Within 30 minutes of his birth (still in my arms in the pool) I would have died for him. I didn't just love him, though, I loved everyone! It was as if I was in a bubble of golden, warm love. I have never felt so high, drugged, or drunk in my life. This is how it should be and this was how it was too for my fourth baby, Violet. No small wonder they are both super-calm and have been from day one. The love for them both was chemical; it was oxytocin . . . and it wasn't there the first two times.

I look at photos of my first two births and my eyes are empty, hollow pools of sadness for the natural births I had lost, and the pain and indignity I had suffered. I didn't feel love; I felt nothing apart from relief it was over maybe and feelings of inadequacy, grief, and confusion that lasted for years after the event. Is it any wonder why so many new mothers find it hard to bond with their baby and hard to interpret their cries, hard to hear their instinct? We strip so many mothers of the natural chemical euphoria they should experience and pay no attention to the after-effects.

The Lasting Psychological Consequences for the Father

It isn't just mothers who can suffer from birth trauma. All too often we forget about the dads, but birth can be—and is—an immensely emotional event for the father, both positively and negatively. Nobody cares about the dads, it seems; nobody holds their hand and tells them they are doing well, and nobody hugs them and listens to their worries or tells them "it's OK" to cry. We expect them to be a tower of strength and support, yet where is the support for them? The sooner we catch onto this problem the better. As a doula I firmly believe my role is 10 percent supporting the mom (if birthing women are left alone in a good environment they pretty much don't need help from me or anyone else) and 90 percent supporting the dad.

When birth goes well it can be an amazing high for the dad too—it can help him bond with his baby almost as instantly as the mom, but when it goes badly. . . . I have been at a few ventouse births and episiotomies now, sitting at "the business end" and sometimes the visions and noises still haunt me and I have witnessed these things before. How must it feel to see your partner in distress, being cut or having a baby pulled out of her with great force? Not really understanding what is happening, feeling helpless, and then being sent home, alone, two hours later if your baby was born outside visiting hours.

We don't seem to appreciate how traumatic witnessing a difficult birth can be for a dad and the impact that can have upon his transition to fatherhood. Indeed we know when dads are supportive of breastfeeding, the mother is much more likely to be successful and feed for longer, but we need to remember that the birth can have a big impact on the dad too, and thus impact massively on the support he is able to give to his partner.

Suggestions for Recovering Psychologically from a Traumatic Birth

Many moms ask me how they can overcome the sadness, guilt, and depression resulting from a traumatic birth. The only thing that really helped me after my first two births was forgiveness and understanding, forgiving myself and those who were with me (and my babies to a lesser extent too) and understanding what happened, why it happened, and why it didn't have to be that way. I knew then that I was not a "failure"; I had BEEN failed. I had been failed by the system and by society; the information I needed was buried because the public were too uncomfortable to discuss it, because the limitations of the system did not allow it.

If we don't discuss the issue of birth trauma, how can we ever change things for future generations; how can we have a better birth next time if we keep burying the truth because it hurts? I know it hurts, but if we want to change we have to discuss it, we have to make peace with what happened, and most importantly of all we need to forgive ourselves. I would like to devote the rest of this chapter to the little things that have helped me and some of the parents I have worked with recover emotionally from a traumatic birth. I have no scientific evidence to share here, only anecdote, but I hope you will find our experiences helpful.

Talk, Talk, Talk . . . and Then Talk Some More

Nobody wanted to listen to me after my first traumatic birth; actually I'm not sure if others even believed the experience *was* traumatic. I was met with so many "but at least he's here safely, that's all that matters" comments that I felt so selfish wanting to yell, "No—it's not all that matters! What about me?" so I never said it, although I wanted to, for so long. In my work with new mothers I've encouraged many to say those things to me, to let those feelings out, and to admit them to themselves. Birth matters. It is not "just one day in your life." Birth can shape your personality for ever more; if it goes well it can change your life leaving you on a euphoric high for years afterwards. If it goes badly it can drag you down for months and even years after the birth and have a lasting impact on your relationship with your baby.

Find somebody you can talk to, somebody who you can trust, somebody who is a good listener, rather than somebody who will frequently interject and offer you their opinion and advice. Many hospitals now employ birth afterthoughts counselors or midwives who will happily go through your notes with you and explain what happened. If you can't find somebody to talk to in person then several organizations offer support over the telephone. At first talking about the birth will hurt—a lot; you'll cry, you'll feel sad, you'll feel angry, you'll feel bitter, you may even feel worse for talking about it, but after a while it will get easier and will really begin to help. It's also really important to talk to your partner about the birth; he himself may be harboring feelings preventing him from bonding too!

Write Your Birth Story

We tend to only write our birth stories if they are positive, but it's so much more important to write out a negative one. You don't have to show it to anyone; indeed, sometimes it can be hugely cathartic to write it out then tear it up—or even burn it. Getting your thoughts down onto paper can be very therapeutic, otherwise why do so many people keep personal journals? A sheet of paper is a very good listener!

Recreate Your Perfect Birth

The idea of recreating your perfect birth or rebirthing may seem strange but it can be amazingly cathartic and can go beyond helping emotional wounds. It can work wonders for helping babies to latch on if you are having trouble and want to breastfeed. I find rebirthing works particularly well for home birth hospital transfers and emergency C-Sections.

I once helped a couple who had planned a home water-birth, which resulted in an emergency C-Section after a long drawn-out labor and an emergency transfer to the hospital, to create positive memories and enjoy the birth environment they so wanted. A week after the birth we set up their birthing room again. It was a crisp winter's evening; we turned up the heating so it was snugly warm, and we got out their birth pool and filled it with warm water. We burned lavender and clary sage oil, we lit candles, we drank wine, we ate fruit, and we played soft music. The mother entered the pool—closed her eyes and floated for a while as dad undressed the baby.

The baby was then gently lowered on to the mom's tummy (with his head out of the water) and then we sat back, in silence, and a beautiful scene unfolded. The baby slowly crawled up and attached onto the mom's breast (this is a technique often recommended for latching problems after C-Sections), and as he did the mom sobbed and sobbed and sobbed—a week's worth of tears. They stayed there for an hour before retreating to bed together, skin to skin, for the night. It will never replace the birth she lost and so wanted, but now she also has good memories too.

Enjoy Skin-to-Skin Contact

I know I've mentioned this subject many times, but again I cannot stress enough the importance and profound benefits of spending time with your baby skin to skin. In my BabyCalm™ classes I always start class two with asking the moms to undress their babies, hold them tight, and close their eyes. I then ask them to feel every last inch of their baby, knowing them through their touch.

I remember the most profound effect I witnessed—a mom with a four-week old, her second baby, who started crying within a minute of doing this. She had been so rushed with her toddler and putting the baby in a sling to get out and about, putting the baby down so the toddler didn't get jealous, and so on, she hadn't had time to get to know her newborn—even though she had had a "perfect" birth (in her words). She said this was the first time she had really touched her baby. Co-bathing is a great time for skin to skin as is co-sleeping; snuggle up with a blanket with your baby stripped down to their diaper and cuddle.

Skin-to-skin contact is really important for bottle feeding moms. Breastfeeding naturally affords skin-to-skin contact many times per day but I don't know of any bottle feeding mom who undoes her shirt and snuggles her baby skin to skin while giving a bottle. It is definitely worth trying, and there's absolutely no reason why you shouldn't share that same physical contact just because you feed your baby by a different method.

Try Babywearing and Co-Sleeping

Babywearing lets you have as much contact as possible with your baby as often as possible. For much more on this look back to chapters 3 and 4.

Avoid Scented Toiletries

All mammals rely strongly on scent to bond with their offspring; we are the only mammals who strip our young of their natural scent and replace it with artificial smells (even if those smells are natural in origin, such as lavender, they are not natural to our babies). Don't underestimate the importance of your baby's natural scent in the early days. Leave the shampoo, baby wash, baby soap, powder, moisturizer, and baby wipes, and stick to plain water as much as possible, as little as possible, particularly on the head, the place where mothers subconsciously nuzzle and sniff many times per day.

Your baby will much prefer your natural smell to that of your scented shower gel, bubble bath, or perfume.

Use Some Psychological Techniques

Hypnosis, neuro-linguistic programming (NLP), visualization, and affirmations are all techniques that can be used to great effect to help encourage bonding and recovery from a difficult birth. I particularly favor an NLP technique called "the swish," which is highly effective and can be easily found online.

Alternatively, something as simple as simply visualizing feelings of love, happiness, and confidence-building when with your baby or repeating statements such as "each day I feel my confidence growing and my love for my baby building" (yes, you do feel stupid at first) can have profound effects. You can visit a hypnotherapist or, for a fraction of the cost, you can buy a CD offering hypnosis for bonding and affirmations for confidence as a new mother.

What Are Hypnotherapy And NLP?

Hypnosis is a very natural state, similar to deep relaxation, driving on autopilot or having a daydream. In this deeply relaxed state we are less critical and more open to new ways of thinking. Lots of people worry that hypnotherapy will be similar to stage hypnosis or what you might have seen on TV, but this is not the case. With hypnotherapy you are in complete control and any hypnosis is self-hypnosis; it is not something that is done to you—you are merely guided by the therapist or the CD you are listening to. It is not spiritual in any sense; it is just a naturally relaxed state of mind. Nobody can make you do anything you do not want to do while in hypnosis and you will remain alert and lucid throughout the whole experience, just very calm.

NLP (neuro-linguistic programming) is a way of understanding and changing a person's thoughts and feelings in order to achieve a more positive outcome. One of the key beliefs of NLP is the idea that we form our own internal mental maps of the world as a product of the world around us due to the way we filter and perceive information absorbed through our senses. In the case of a negative birth experience NLP can be used to alter our maps of the experience to remove some of the hurtful feelings and leave us more able to move on from the experience with positivity.

A visit to a hypnotherapist or NLP practitioner or listening to a CD can be very healing after a traumatic birth and can really help to ease your transition into motherhood.

Give It Time

They say time is the greatest healer, so don't rush yourself, it will only make you feel more guilty. You've proved what a great mother you are already by recognizing the issue and wanting to change, so a change will happen, indeed it has already happened by just admitting to yourself. That change might not be instant, particularly if you are having first to go through a grief process. Time, acceptance, and understanding were what helped me the most after my traumatic births, but I would be lying if I said, even ten years on, that I didn't have the odd stab of regret or pang of guilt.

So what do I do with the information that is given to me about their birth experiences from the new parents in my BabyCalm™ classes? Most of the time I do nothing. Sometimes I'll suggest a visit to a chiropractor, breastfeeding counselor, or birth afterthoughts midwife, or a telephone call to the Birth Trauma Association, but rarely. I listen and I listen some more. For that mom or dad it may be the first time somebody has listened and we should never underestimate the impact that feeling listened to can have on somebody's state of mind. Birth matters and you matter, so give yourself the time and get the help and support that you need, for when you take care of yourself you can take much better care of your new family.

Katherine's Story

My daughter's birth was not a great one. Unfortunately my little girl came like a lightning bolt, and in the confusion of being told that I was not in labor when in fact I was, I went into a massive panic and had a natural, but very scary and terribly painful birth, which resulted in a third-degree tear. After being taken away to another room and sewn up for an hour straight after birth I felt cruelly robbed of my skin-to-skin cuddling and bonding time. My husband, of course, was with my little girl, shirt undone, holding her close, and I was thankful for their shared moments, but ultimately I felt robbed. After finally returning to my room I found my little girl bundled up like a beautiful yet surreal little doll in a plastic crib. It was midnight by that point and after helping me with a shower, my husband (and the hospital it seemed) went home for the night. I spent the night staring at my little girl, too full of adrenaline and shock to sleep, yet in too much pain to pick her up. I cried for six hours solid that night; I felt scared, depressed, and empty. I ached to hold her, but not having the strength or confidence to do so, I made do with arranging soft cuddly toys around her and sat and stared, and missed how close we were when she was inside me.

When we got her home I had the same sense of separation. The first night I put her in her little crib beside our bed, every part of me felt wrong. Every noise she made seemed alien and heart-breaking. I couldn't close my eyes for fear that she would stop breathing and be taken away from me. I felt fiercely protective, but without her being inside me I felt as if I had lost my power of protection. The inches of darkness between us, the cold Moses basket, the blanket, and everything around her seemed to pose a threat to her. It was as if the safety of our bedroom had become a death trap of man-eating beasts. I knew I was being irrational but I could not sleep and nor could she.

As the weeks went on Evie would only sleep in someone's arms and if she did sleep in a Moses basket she would make the most dreadful fitful noises and I would lightly doze on the edge of the sofa so that I could see inside the Moses basket and hold her as I tried to sleep. Every noise that she made, I felt like she was going to stop breathing, I must have checked her chest virtually every 20 minutes for those first two months. I became sleep deprived and depressed. I had become a mom and yet all I seemed to have was a neurotic feeling of not being close enough to my daughter, and not being good enough to be able to protect her and help her sleep. I resented her for my lack of sleep and desperately wanted to feel at peace and in love with my little girl.

Looking back on these bleak, sleep-deprived times I feel amazed that I had not thought of co-sleeping earlier. I knew all Evie wanted was to feel close like she had when I was pregnant, but my fear for her safety and my lack of knowledge stopped me from trying the one thing that was sure to cure all of our problems. All I could hear was society's warnings of the fact that it was unsafe to sleep with your child; if you slept in the same bed as your baby you would no doubt smother and kill it. I have always been a restless fidget in bed, and with my constant fear of crib death there was no way that I would risk smothering her. So, filled with this fear I spent two and a half months in torment, trying whatever I could to get Evie to sleep out of arms during the day and at night. She cried, I cried, but surely that was my only choice.

Then one ground-breaking and sleep-deprived day I was feeding Evie lying down in bed during the day (the easiest method with my stitches), and lo and behold, we both fell asleep. We slept for about three amazing hours together, which after three months without sleep was like a miracle. Not only that but I hadn't moved in my sleep! Despite being the world's greatest sleep fidget I awoke to find my arms around her and her arms around me. I hadn't rolled, I hadn't pushed her off the edge, and most importantly we had both slept. Not only this, but for the first time since giving birth to her I felt at peace; I felt like a mom and that our bond had finally been renewed in those three hours.

Evie is now ten months; she starts the night in her own crib and then comes in next to me when she wakes up (usually perfectly timed for our bedtime). We use a side guard rail and at the moment everything works really well. No doubt there will be more questions to solve if we are lucky enough for our family to get bigger, but I would now openly and confidently recommend co-sleeping to any parent. For my part it has finally given me back the bond that I feel was taken from me at birth, and for that I will be eternally grateful. My only hope is that co-sleeping can become a real and open option for parents and that it is not left in a shady corner for people to accidentally discover as a last resort.

Chapter 12

The Transition to Motherhood

The moment a child is born, the mother is also born. She never existed before. The woman existed, but the mother, never. A mother is something absolutely new.

—Rajneesh, guru

"What did you do today?" Ask this question to many new mothers and usually they will answer, "Oh nothing" or, "Not much." . . . We don't realize how valuable we, as mothers, are. We don't appreciate what an important role we play and quite how much we do. If we do not value ourselves, how do we ever expect others to value us? I've been thinking a lot about this over the past week as I've chatted with friends with children at home, many of them telling me they are tearing their hair out with boredom, frustration, tiredness, and guilt. They think they should be doing more, they think they should be doing less, they think they have not been a good mother when their children fight with each other, the toddler draws on the wall, or the baby cries all day. Mothers are often their own worst critics.

The Curse of Mommy Guilt

Mommy guilt is one of the worst parts of becoming a mother. Being a mother is hard—really hard—and not just because of the sleepless nights and the constant, never-ending feeding sessions. Perhaps motherhood is hardest of all the very first time you become one, the time of the biggest transition, and the most uprooting change, in the transition from being your old carefree individual self to now having huge responsibility in caring for this tiny new being. You are no longer "me" or "I"; you are now "we" or "us."

More extreme is the fact that you might find you lose your identity even more by losing your name, as you now become known as "Seb's mom," as I have been known for nearly ten years now. Some people I speak to fairly regularly still have absolutely no idea of what my Christian name is. I am no longer "Sarah," not in the sense I was before I had children anyway. Sometimes I don't even know who "Sarah" is any more, as my whole existence is now so intertwined with that of my children.

At first I fought against the change, as so many new mothers do, before I embraced it and welcomed it. Now I would never look back; the "Sarah" I once was may have been able to go out for the evening without worrying about babysitters, creased clothes, baby sick on her shoulder, and un-brushed hair; she may have been able to afford expensive cosmetics, costly haircuts, and designer clothes; she may have been able to read a whole book whenever she wanted or lie by the pool undisturbed for the whole day on vacation, but I have something much, much more valuable. I have children; I have a constant reminder of why we are here; I have limitless love to give and receive and that is so much more than I ever had before—it's just a shame it took me so long to realize it!

With this in mind I would like to set you a challenge, a piece of homework if you like. Tomorrow morning, when you wake, I'd like you to find a piece of paper and a pen and write down everything you do, and I mean everything, all day. That includes anything from changing a diaper to wiping up baby sick, feeding your baby to feeding the dog, loading the dishwasher to paying a bill or shopping for groceries, and it most definitely includes any thought time you've given over to your family, time spent Googling for answers to today's parenting query, and time spent reading this book, because every little thing you do is so worthwhile and so vital to the physiological and psychological wellbeing of your child. You do so much more than you think you do. You have absolutely nothing to feel guilty about and everything to be proud of.

Psychotherapist and author of *What Mothers Do*, Naomi Stadlen also speaks about the importance of "mother worrying," commenting on what a commendable skill it is. Naomi explains how mothers constantly strive for what is best for their family, how they are constantly researching, how they weigh up the pros and cons before making their decision (like many of the most respected business leaders) on a daily basis, yet friends and family members will just say, "Oh, she worries so much," dismissively, like it's a flaw instead of something to be congratulated! Mothers are busy, busy with important work!

With this in mind, tomorrow evening I'd like you to really look at your list and appreciate all that you do, all that you are, because I have no doubt you are amazing, even when you worry so much that you aren't. Be proud of the mother you are and never, ever apologize for your perceived lack of worth; never apologize for the mess your house is in; never apologize for your un-brushed hair, because what you do is worth so much more.

The Bumpy Road of New Motherhood

The road to motherhood can be a short, easy journey for some and for others a mountainous trek, but always it is a journey of great discovery, not just about babies and parenting, but often a wonderful journey of self-discovery. Often for new mothers it can seem as if their whole world is turned upside down; they can often question long-held beliefs and discover emotions that they did not know existed before. Things that once seemed so important suddenly seem trivial. Sometimes, though, motherhood disappoints or throws up many difficult feelings, but don't see these feelings and obstacles as failings—see them as an opportunity to make change tomorrow.

Losing Control

I think one of the hardest things I found about becoming a mother for the first time was the sheer lack of control I felt. I had had a very good job with a large amount of responsibility in a male-dominated world. I got up at the same time every morning and put on my power suit. I drove the same commute every day in my clean and tidy company car, and I had a series of routines to perform at work, all of which I was very much in control of. I got home at the same time each day. I cooked and ate my dinner at the same time. I went grocery shopping every Thursday and clothes shopping every Saturday. I went to yoga on a Tuesday evening. I had a facial every fourth Saturday and a haircut every eight weeks. I always knew what date it was, how much money I had in the bank, and I absolutely always remembered friends' and relatives' birthdays. I was very much in control. Before my firstborn even arrived I had bought every item of clothing he would ever need until age one (neatly folded in drawers and hung on wooden hangers in his freshly painted white wardrobe). I had enough diapers to last for the first three months and enough muslin cloths to clean up the sick of a million babies. Oh yes, I was in control and then some.

Then he arrived . . . and almost instantly I had no control. How could something so small be so much more demanding than my previous professional life? I was used to giving boardroom presentations, flying to Switzerland at the drop of a hat, and commissioning research worth more money than I will ever see in my lifetime, yet I was floored by this small bundle. Overnight my life became a blur of diaper changing, feeding, and rocking. I didn't know what day of the week it was, let alone the date. Occasionally I forgot what month and even year it was too. Any routine I had went instantly out of the window, so the lure to recreate a routine was strong, particularly as that was what was advocated so strongly by the magazines, books, and internet sites I read. I was tempted and even tried a few routines for a couple of days, but they just didn't sit well with either me or Seb. The difference was before I became a mother I lived to my routine, so following somebody else's rigid routine felt just as alien to me as being thrown into routine-free chaos. Seb reacted as strongly as I did; he didn't like being told when he could eat, drink, sleep, and play and made his distaste obvious through his tears.

For us the key was to embrace this new way of life. I'm not denying it was hard in the beginning, but slowly I began to love the calmer pace of our days. Surprisingly, as Seb reached three months old he developed his own patterns; he would wake and feed at 7 AM, have another feed at 10 AM, and then sleep until lunchtime, I could almost set my watch by him. Remarkably, though, he had fallen into this pattern all by himself; he had found his own routine and so too had I regained some control back in my life, without controlling his.

I never did try to control life with any of my subsequent babies. Often people say to me, "Wow, four kids and a business, how do you do it? What's your secret?" I always tell them I have no secret, but really when I think about it more I think the secret is to embrace the changes, go with the flow, and relax a little. Motherhood has indeed changed me, but now I can say I firmly believe it has all been for the better.

The Amazing, Difficult, and Surprising Parts of New Motherhood

In my research for this book I asked several new mothers about their experiences of new motherhood and particularly what parts they had found amazing, surprising, and hard. These were some of their responses:

> It changed everything about me. Even the things I didn't know needed changing. I could never go back now.

> I found the lack of control hard. I was used to being in control of all areas of my life but once I just stopped trying to run to an agenda and just went with it I loved it! What surprised me was how hard the first few weeks are. Also the overwhelming love I feel for my baby, which means that nothing else is important. He is my life and my entire focus. I have no idea what I did before he came along!

> Nothing could have prepared me for the love that I felt. It's not like the love you feel for a partner, brother, sister, mother, or father. It's indescribable.

> I loved being a mommy from the first time that I saw my baby girl! It is the best feeling in the world being a mommy. I thought that breastfeeding was going to be easy, but I learned that it wasn't easy at all for me. I was also surprised that everything just came to me naturally. I was so afraid that I wasn't going to know what to do when she arrived, but I'm doing perfectly fine.

I found it very hard to cope with the loss of control of my time, as I am a very organized person (or try to be). I felt very scared when I had my baby, as I had not really had much to do with babies before. My initial reaction was "What the hell do I do now? . . . Mom, help me!" I didn't want my mom to go home, I felt quite terror stricken. I pored over endless books telling you what to do, but each seemed different so I Googled it, which also led to thousands of different comments. I just wanted someone to hand me an instruction manual. It took a good few months to feel like being a mother was "normal life" for me, but now eighteen months on I love my son so much I can't believe something so cute and gorgeous was half created by me.

That moment you first hold your baby is like nothing else on this earth. I remember people telling me that but you can never really be prepared for that wonderful feeling that hits you so hard and I sometimes panic that I will wake up one day and won't be able to remember it! The one thing I was definitely not prepared for was the constant guilt that seemed to come with having a baby, when you don't feel sure if you're doing it right. There are so many ways of doing things and every mother and child is different and I found it hard (and still do) to not question if someone else's way was the better way: "Maybe I should have done it like that . . . "; "what if I had done this. . . . " I envy the mothers who seem confident with every decision they make and those with the conviction that their way is the best way, but I just have to accept that being unsure initially and questioning everything obviously is my way and I will always get there in the end. Having my babies is the one thing that I have done in my life that I am truly proud of.

Good parts: lying in bed staring at beautiful baby, watching a lot of TV! Bad parts: feeling a bit lonely and losing track of what was going on in the world.

Returning to Work or Staying at Home

For many mothers maternity leave is often bittersweet. Just as they begin to really enjoy staying at home with their baby so they must return to work and leave them. Some mothers I have met have chosen to make great sacrifices in their life in order to stay at home with their babies, downsizing houses, selling cars, forgoing holidays, curtailing social lives, and the like, such is their need to stay close to their babies.

Some feel they will be better mothers if they return to work, keeping their minds active and spending time away from their baby in order to return to him with renewed energy and enthusiasm at the end of the day. Others simply don't have any choice financially but to return to work. One thing is for sure, whichever choice you make you will feel guilty. You might sometimes feel jealous of the mothers who do different than you and there will always be days that you wish you had made the opposite choice. Such is the life of a twenty-first-century mother; not only do we have to settle in to life as a new mother, we often have to balance it with many other jobs too, often with little help from nearby family members, unlike our predecessors. We are expected not only to balance these roles with ease; we are expected to excel at them all while also being a "yummy mummy" (how I hate that phrase). No wonder postnatal depression is so common. We are not superhuman and nor should we try to be, for that is where the problems lie.

I asked several mothers how they felt about returning to work after maternity leave during the course of writing this book, and here are just a handful of their responses:

I went back to work when Rosa was two-and-a-half months old, because she was such a good sleeper and so calm, I was going a bit stir crazy. It was horrible not being with her, though; there are negatives and positives both to going back to work and staying at home.

I had kept in touch with work regularly throughout my maternity leave and was lucky to be returning to a very supportive team, so the first day wasn't too painful! However, despite emails weeks in advance letting HR know I would be expressing breast milk at work, there were no facilities provided and I ended up expressing in a committee room! Later I was told to express in a public "quiet room," which culminated a couple of weeks later in me being barged in on by a very angry gentleman mid-expressing. Not the best advert for promoting breastfeeding, as my employer claims to do! However, the actual return has been quite smooth, despite changing jobs two weeks after going back. Coming back part time definitely helped.

The week before I built it up to be this huge heartbreaking thing, the guilt was awful, even with my parents having her, two people I trust implicitly. Walking back into that office in the City was so nerve-wracking but the end of the day honestly did come in a flash and the lunch break was a luxury. Of course my baby had a lovely time! I was lucky though; I only worked two days a week. I couldn't imagine doing any more and was lucky not to have to.

Postnatal Depression

Around 15 percent of mothers will suffer from postnatal depression (PND). It is incredibly common and absolutely nothing to be embarrassed about or ashamed of. Sometimes there is an obvious reason for the depression, such as a difficult pregnancy or a traumatic birth, or there can be no obvious reason whatsoever. Sometimes mothers are afraid to seek the help they need as they are worried about admitting that they are not coping, afraid that others will see them as a failure or, at worst, incapable of looking after their baby.

Anybody can suffer from PND. It is nobody's fault; it doesn't depend on your age, your income, your education, your nationality, or whether this is your first child or your fifth. PND is not selective in who it chooses to visit. PND usually starts within the first two months of having your baby, but it can also start several months afterwards. Depression can also start during pregnancy (antenatal depression) and continue after the birth; indeed this usually happens to around one-third of the women suffering from PND. PND can also affect men.

Symptoms of Postnatal Depression

- Feeling depressed, sad, and tearful
- Feeling exhausted
- Being unable to sleep (particularly given the above)
- Being very irritable
- Feeling apathetic, losing interest in things
- A feeling of not enjoying being with your baby
- Lack of libido
- Losing your appetite or overly comfort eating
- Feeling overly guilty
- Lacking confidence
- Feeling unable to cope
- Anxiety—particularly over your baby's health and wellbeing
- Panic attacks
- Withdrawing from society, wanting to stay home all of the time
- Feelings of hopelessness

If you feel that these symptoms could describe how you are feeling please do seek help. I didn't when I experienced them with my second baby; I faked the test my health visitor asked me to complete. I knew which answers were "good" and which were "bad," so I lied. I lied to everybody as I felt too ashamed to admit I wasn't coping; I don't know why. To this day this is one of my biggest regrets as a mother. I have very little recollection of the first year of my second's son life, and as a result I lost friends and alienated myself from many people I cared for. None of that needed to have happened if I'd only sought the help I required. I cannot urge you strongly enough to seek help if you even have the tiniest suspicion that you may have PND.

I often think that PND is so common because of the comparative lack of support available to new mothers, added to the burden of being a perfect mother and the myriad of expert "how to" baby manuals. I'm actually quite surprised that the figure is as low as 15 percent. For many the first step towards a recovery is admitting to yourself that something is not quite right and the second is seeking help. That help may come in the form of confiding in a trusted friend or family member, calling a national helpline, or most commonly visiting your GP or health visitor. If your PND is mild, often just creating a support network through friends and family and perhaps enlisting help from a postnatal doula (see box) could be enough to help you cope, but if your PND is more severe you will need more help, which your doctor can help you to get. Whatever route you take you should not be embarrassed, but know that you are doing your best for your baby by seeking the help you need to be a good mom. You matter too.

Motherless Mothers

An increasing number of mothers are giving birth without the help and support of their own mother, maybe because she lives many miles away, maybe because her own mother died before she became a mother herself, or for some their relationship with their own mother has broken down, often irreconcilably.

What Is A Postnatal Doula?

The word *doula* (pronounced doo-la) comes from Greek, and refers to "a woman of service" or even "slave." A doula is usually an experienced mother herself who has usually undertaken some initial training followed by a period of mentoring. A doula aims to support a new mother. She will never tell the mother what to do, but rather will help her to explore her new role, act as a listening ear or sounding board, and provide information to help a new mother to care for her baby with confidence. On top of this a postnatal doula will often cook and clean for the new mother and generally pamper her so that she can enjoy her babymoon, whether that be by holding the baby while the mom takes a long soak in the bath, walking the dog, or entertaining an elder sibling so that the mom and new baby may bond in peace.

For many women becoming a mother can often raise queries over our own mothering and upbringing; for some it can cause friction with their own mother and bring up doubts or queries about their childhood. For some mothers, too, it can be a hard experience watching your daughter become a mother, particularly if her way of doing things is different to the way she was brought up, causing you to re-evaluate the way you parented.

My own mother died from breast cancer when I was twenty-one and she was only fifty-two years old. Five years later, I gave birth to my first baby and became a "motherless mother." My own personal journey as a mother has therefore been bittersweet. I have loved finding a new dimension to myself, I have loved watching my children grow and am continually amazed by them, I have loved viewing the world with fresh vision through their eyes, but I realize now quite how much I have lost. For it is only now I realize the true depth of feelings my mother had towards me, how much of herself she sacrificed for me in the years she stayed at home to raise me and I wish I could say "thank you." I wish I could ask how motherhood was for her. I wish she could meet my children; I wish she could bake cakes with my boys and make paper flowers with my daughter like she did with me. I wish she could read them the bedtime stories I loved so much from the very same books that now sit in my daughter's bedroom. I wish I could ask her about her pregnancy with me, about my own birth, and my early days of babyhood. In becoming a mother I am starkly reminded of quite how much I have lost with the passing of my own mother in a way that I never mourned before I had my own children.

Although I often say I now feel complete since having children, in many ways I feel far less than a whole. I am a mother now, a wife, a friend, and more, but I am no longer a child to anybody (my father died three years after my mother, two years before I became a mother) and only now do I realize the importance of that dynamic and the sharing of parenting wisdom through generations.

In her book *Motherless Mothers, How Mother Loss Shapes the Parents We Become*, Hope Edelman discusses her experiences of mothering without a mother, in particular how she believes that motherless mothers often face unique anxieties. In her book she quotes psychotherapist Irene Rubaum-Keller as saying, "It takes a lot of courage for motherless daughters to have kids . . . because it is a means of saying, 'We're going to live.'" I think it is perfectly normal, and very common, for all mothers to worry about the future and what would happen to their children if they were no longer around. For the motherless mother, though, this anxiety is much heightened, due to their experience of losing their own mother, for many therefore they carry the extra anxiety of "What happens if I die young too?" into their mothering journey.

I also realize that many mothers may feel too that they are motherless in a way, even though their mother may still be alive. I actually feel more fortunate than these women, as I feel incredibly lucky for the close and sharing relationship I had with my mother when she was still here, while some I know spend their whole life seeking that closeness from a mother, still alive, who is for some reason or other unable to give it. I know many whose mothers are still alive who have never experienced that bond, and for some their lack of relationship with their own mother now that they have become a mother themselves may be harder to bear than if she were actually dead. Many find themselves becoming mothers when their own mothers are geographically very far away, sometimes even on the other side of the world, and this can also be incredibly hard.

It Takes a Village to Raise a Child

Society has lost value in maternal roles; we have lost value in grandmothers, great-grandmothers, and in those feminine feet who walked in our footsteps before us too. We have lost value in female knowledge and the family in the raising of a child. Our society is so masculine, so materialistic, and so authoritarian; it is almost as if we are afraid to be feminine, to be soft, and to be mothers. We have lost our way; we all need a maternal influence, whatever our age, whoever we are.

A few years ago I read *The Red Tent* by Anita Diamant—a wonderful story, set in biblical times, detailing the lives of a group of women—and thought wistfully of a society so primitive, masculine, and blood-thirsty and yet quietly run and steered by a deep feminine and maternal presence. I thought about how amazing it would be to live and parent in a world of such sisterhood, understanding, and acceptance. How do we return to this ethos? How can we once again hold the matriarchs dear and close at the head of society? In many parts of the world they still are, so why not in the West? How much of a difference would it make to our own parenting journey if we were aided by the close support of our own mothers, grandmothers, sisters, cousins, aunts, and friends? To quote the famous African proverb, "It takes a village to raise a child." I believe this lack of "village" support is part of what makes mothering so hard. In some ways we at BabyCalm™ are aiming to replicate these "villages" and their support, with our teachers, classes, and groups.

The "Good Enough" Mother

The British pediatrician, child psychiatrist, and psychoanalyst Donald Winnicott coined the phrase "the good enough mother" over sixty years ago, but it is still a concept well worth discussing today. What makes a perfect mother? What makes a bad mother? What makes a "good enough" mother? Why do we place pressure on ourselves to strive for perfection when we can be "good enough"?

Winnicott described the "good enough" mother as:

> A mother is neither good nor bad nor the product of illusion, but is a separate and independent entity: The good-enough mother . . . starts off with an almost complete adaptation to her infant's needs, and as time proceeds she adapts less and less completely, gradually, according to the infant's growing ability to deal with her failure. Her failure to adapt to every need of the child helps them adapt to external realities.

As such Winnicott believes that the "good enough" mother is actually better than a perfect mother; perfect mothers, he believed, can even be harmful. What does a "good enough" mother do, though? First she allows her baby to attach to her as much as the baby needs; as such she provides a safe base, a "holding environment" as Winnicott calls it, from which he can explore the world. When a baby is young this is the role of the "good enough" mother, to hold her baby and help him to feel secure. As the baby grows he can begin to leave the mother with his growing independence; the "good enough" mother's role here is to simply allow the baby this freedom, nothing more, nothing less. By not trying to be perfect, through her mistakes and challenges, the mother creates a more emotionally healthy baby; she is just enough for him. She is a "good enough mother." Just as you, too, are a "good enough" mother: I hope that you believe that now.

Corinne's Story

My parents and sister (and her two children) live in New Zealand and my husband's parents live 200 miles away from us.

I feel I have it easy compared to my own mom: she met my dad in New Zealand while on a working holiday from the UK. When we were born she would take one or two photos a month of my sister and I to send to her mother in the UK, but Granny would have to wait until the end of the roll of film before receiving the photos, meaning it could be a year between sets of photos. They exchanged one letter a week. In comparison, we phoned my parents within an hour of birthing, emailed photos any time we wanted, and exchanged weekly Skype video chats. The video conversations have meant that my son has a strong attachment to his Granny, which is wonderful, especially when we visit in person.

Skype did us a great service as new parents—visits from family and friends were easily delayed for the first week by video calls, leaving us in peace to get to know our baby and for me to get the hang of breastfeeding. By the time we welcomed visitors into our home I was feeding confidently and my husband had quickly noticed our baby's early hungry cues (sniffing). When my parents visited between four to eight weeks after the birth, my mom—a 1960s Great Ormond Street Hospital trained pediatric nurse and midwife—observed that my "cue feeding" was very different to the feeding advice she'd been trained to give mothers, which was no more frequently than every four hours!

I feel lucky that I found a knowledgeable, supportive online community of mothers from whom I gleaned loads of information about mothering, especially how all babies are different. I'd read many mothers' stories of difficulty; and the answers to the "silly" questions others more brave than me had asked. This gave me confidence that there were things I could do for my baby, but if these didn't work then there were other things I could try; there were trusted people online to ask for suggestions; there were trust-worthy websites full of evidence-based information from which I could make informed choices (I'm a scientist so these really appealed). I was very lucky to have this congregation of motherhood with its vast collection of experiences to inform my choices. Despite this, I was still worried I wouldn't cope if I got a high-needs baby who cried lots, so my first baby-preparation purchases included a sling or two.

My mothering choices have differed quite a bit from my immediate family; I wasn't aware of this for months, so being distant from family has benefits! My sister is much-less evidence-based than me, and she's firmly in the early sleep-training camp so we're complete opposites there; my mom was very skeptical of baby-led weaning (BLW) but her alarmed expressions when I described the principles of BLW during Skype chats were easy to ignore (Mom was converted when she saw BLW in action during our visit at nine to ten months). My mother-in-law has a wonderful understanding of the benefits of being baby-led, and every mother's right to make her own choices.

Mothering at a distance from family has meant long-haul travel and long-term stays (often from three to five weeks). These are very intensive periods where I have sometimes felt bombarded by a year's worth of disapproval all at once. Where I have looked forward to some respite from the continual demands of mothering, I have returned feeling more emotionally exhausted. On a more practical note, long-haul flights always go much better than I expect—breastfeeding and slings have been my absolute saviors.

Imogen's Story

When I was asked to share my story, I wasn't sure how to start. It doesn't often feel as though there is a "story" to tell as such; it's just part of my life.

My mother passed away after a year-long battle with cancer when I was sixteen years old. Life changed in a huge way and promised to never be the same again. We lived alone, the pair of us, so I had to learn not only how to function in a new reality without the safety of my mother, but how to function as an adult alone—cleaning, cooking, paying bills, and being responsible. As you can imagine, it was a period of huge adjustment and saw me going off the rails for a while.

Fast-forward three years and I had found my way back, and was pregnant with my first child. The pregnancy was planned, but I was still terrified. Many people asked me if it was hard, expecting a child without having my own mother there to help, and in all honesty I kind of brushed it off. When people offered their sympathy, telling me they never could have coped without their moms, I shrugged and simply thought, well, I have nothing to compare it to, this is my reality, and this is what I have to deal with.

I was aware at the time that not having your mother around was a risk factor for PND, and along with several other risk factors I possessed, I knew my chances of avoiding it were slim. Much to my dismay I did not avoid it, and the first year of my son's life was plagued with the crippling disease. When I look back at his baby days, I feel cold and want to cry.

Two years later, I fell pregnant with my second baby after two early miscarriages. I did not escape the dreaded PND this time either, but thankfully it did not affect the bond with my baby in the same way as it did the first time around. It did take longer to be diagnosed; it was one of those evil bouts of depression that you don't notice until it sucks you right under.

Thankfully, medication has helped me immensely during both episodes of PND.

I haven't ever openly said this to anybody, but, yes— not having my own mother around while raising my children has been very, very hard. There's often a sense of unfairness about the whole thing. I feel as though I have been robbed of the mother–daughter bonding experience that others get to have when they have their own babies. I've watched my friends' relationships with their mothers blossom and become more profound as they become mothers themselves, and it hurts that I never had a chance to have that with my mom.

I feel angry that the little things my peers take for granted are things I will never experience, and I feel sad for my babies that they will never know their amazing grandmother. Of course, they'll know her through me, but they won't know her first hand like I was lucky enough to. When I hear of mothers moaning about their parents for interfering with the way they are raising their children, I feel a strange mix of empathy and frustration. It must be hard to deal with that, but at least you have your mom, I petulantly think.

Another thing that I find myself thinking about often is how different my life would have been if it weren't for losing my mom at such a critical, pivotal age. When she died, I felt I had no choice but to drop out of school. I needed to learn how to run a home, and I needed to earn money with which to do so—finishing my A levels was not an option. My family and children are most definitely the silver lining of losing my mom—after all, I wouldn't have met my husband had things been different—but in my lowest depressive moments, when I've been overwhelmed with responsibility and full of resentment for the small people that heap that responsibility on my shoulders, I've grieved for the life that I could have had. I've grieved for the experiences I missed out on and the freedom I should have reveled in, instead of desperately searching for some way to fill the gaping hole that losing my mom left in the pit of my stomach. Losing weight and partying way too hard didn't fill it, and neither did having children of my own (although the joy they bring me comes damn close sometimes).

I think one of the most frustrating things about mothering when you are motherless, and the thing that ties all the other things together, is that childish feeling of it's not fair. I am one of the lucky ones—I don't have my mother, but I have a supportive father, a wonderful family-in-law, a husband who any woman would be lucky to have, and a group of amazing friends. Many don't have that. But I still find myself wishing that I had my mom here—not just to support me through the hard times, but to share the good times with, too. When you lose your mother before you should have done, it's easy to find yourself regressing to the sulky teenager within who feels so damn hard done by even with plenty to be grateful for.

Sian's Story

For a lot of his first year, I have found dealing with my son David really, really hard, mostly because of sleep deprivation. Technically David was a "good" baby; he mostly slept in the night in three- or four-hour stretches, and those got longer as he got older, but I still found the disrupted sleep patterns very hard to cope with, and for a long time felt he completely destroyed any semblance of quality of life that I had. For as much as up to nine months after his birth I felt like I was sort of stuck. I found that I had a lot of conflicting emotions around being somebody's mother, but I found it really difficult to talk about any of it for fear that any of the slightest suggestion that maybe I don't love everything about being a mother would be indicative of me not coping. The concept of demonstrating "coping" was very important to me for a long time. I was terrified people would think I had not formed enough of a bond with my child.

Basically, I think it boils down to the fact that this baby stuff is HARD. It's much harder than I thought it was going to be, and that's because I don't think anything can actually prepare you for the full-on relentlessness of it. People told me it would be hard beforehand, but in the way someone can tell you a curry is spicy before you bite it; you only know once you've taken a mouthful how hot you find it to be. The problem is to say that child rearing is hard is expected, but to say you're not enjoying it is perceived to be an appalling affront to the very heart of motherhood.

But there's the other side of the coin, because while, on the one hand, it is unrelenting toil, it's also lovely. There's a tiny little chap who wriggles around the floor and sticks inappropriate things in his mouth and learns all the time and is really happy to see you and lifts up his little hands so you'll pick him up and who you love with an extraordinary intensity. I don't find it boring, not all the time.

I like his enthusiasm for sticking things in his mouth, I am amused by the faces he makes, by him smearing himself in spoon-food, and by the damage four teeth could do to a slice of cucumber and the destruction eight teeth can wreak on an apple. But some days, playing with blocks is still playing with blocks, and I'm a bit old for it to be truly stimulating. It took me a long, long time to begin to feel comfortable even hinting at all this. I was terrified my family and friends would think I didn't love David and that I was a bad mother. And while it shouldn't matter what others think, to be honest, it does matter to most of us.

In the end, I did manage to climb out of my rut, and what other people think of me matters less now. Three things really helped me, and I started doing them at the same time when David was about eight months old. My parents had been asking if they could buy us something for ages, so I asked if they would get us a baby carrier. Using that, I started going on little hikes across the countryside at least once a week. If we were in the house he was as busy as any baby, keen to explore and get into everything, but when he was in the sling he rarely cried, and more often than not he just quieted down and went to sleep. For me, I got that space of quiet, to think about what I want, or, even better, think about nothing at all. Sometimes I walk with friends, but sometimes I don't want that. Sometimes I just want the time to think quietly. I once heard someone describe staying at home with your baby as "being alone without the benefits of solitude." What walking did was give me back a space to think. If he's in his sling, he's either entertained by the view or asleep, and what I get is some peace. While I can't guarantee that I will get to the end of my cup of tea without the baby wanting me to do something, I can pretty much be sure of getting to the end of the walk without him interfering with my thought processes.

The other thing I did was to start blogging about these hikes. Lots of my friends said they wanted to go for walks but just kept going walking in the same places, so I started to write about where I went and what I thought about while I was going. After a while, I got up the courage to put a link on Facebook when the blog updated, so my friends could read what I was doing. The response I got was hugely encouraging, in the distance that the internet affords, people were able to pop up on Facebook or leave a comment on the blog and say to me "yes, yes I felt that too," and that has really helped my sanity. And let's face it; sanity can wear pretty thin when you've been woken up at 12 AM, 3 AM, and 6 AM for months on end.

From that, I had the confidence to go out and join a "sling Meet" and get to know other mothers who were going about raising their children in a manner similar to the way I was doing it. I hadn't known any babywearers or baby-led-weaners before, so to find other people who were doing the same things as I was felt reassuring, and finally, finally I felt I had found my feet as a parent, and could identify myself as being both a person and a mother.

Alex's Story

Our first baby was born in New Zealand, where my husband is from. When I moved there I didn't know anyone except my husband, and his family lived several hours away from us.

Immediately after our first baby was born my mom came to stay for three weeks, which was great as she and I have a very close relationship and having her around to help with cooking, cleaning, washing, etc. allowed me to really take things easy, establish breastfeeding, and get to know my baby. I also really found that her emotional support during this time was so valuable; I had no experience of babies at all and felt very lost. Nothing had prepared me for life as a mother. In hindsight, though, it may have been better if she had come to stay after my husband went back to work because it was a bit of a shock to be suddenly home alone.

Luckily I had made friends with several of the ladies in our antenatal classes. We met as a group often and I would have coffee with two of them several times a week. I became close with those two and when my husband had to frequently go away on long courses/deployments (he is in the army), they would invite me and the baby over for dinner and even to stay the night. Shortly after my son was born, I started going to La Leche League meetings, which were weekly. The ladies I met there became some of the best and most supportive friends I have ever had. It amazed me how within moments of meeting other mothers, they were inviting us for tea, arranging visits, and even offering to come and watch the baby so I could catch up on some sleep! It really made things easier, having friends to call and visit when I was alone for long periods.

I think the secret to my survival as a new mother was having such amazing, supportive friends. I think if someone offers you support, help, or friendship, even if you haven't known them long, it's really important to grab it with both hands. I have found that great friendships are built quickly in difficult times. People generally don't offer help unless they genuinely want to be supportive and it is guaranteed to make you feel human again. And they really don't care if your house is a mess. The other thing that I found quite sanity-saving during the weeks on my own, was that my mom would ring me after work every night, which for me was breakfast time. We would talk about everything and anything and I would really look forward to her calls.

When our second baby was born, we were living in the UK. My husband was reposted and the army moved us when our son was just four weeks old. We moved to a town that I had never even visited, and we didn't know anyone. With a newborn baby and a preschooler, in a new town, I found life extremely difficult. My husband was deployed for four months shortly after we moved and I really struggled to get out of the house. Something that I have found strangely helpful is using Facebook to stay in touch with friends; especially the amazing ladies back in New Zealand. It's amazing how connected and rejuvenated you can feel when people show their love and support for you via social networking! I actually hate how much I use it but there are times when I feel so lonely—despite being overwhelmed by the company of my small children—that I would give anything to have someone to sit and talk rubbish to, and I think you do get that a bit with social networking, in a weird sort of way.

The hardest part of the day for me, when my husband is away, is at about 5 PM. Obviously, to be at home with the kids during the day is normal, but every day when I begin to make dinner it suddenly dawns on me that he won't be walking through the door soon. The realization that I have to do dinner, bath time, bedtime all on my own, again, never gets any easier. Similarly weekends are always really hard. Even when you do have lots of friends around, on the weekends everyone tends to be busy with their own family stuff, but the "groundhog day" feeling of everyday life doesn't go away at the weekend when you're on your own with children for weeks/months on end.

The BabyCalm™ Maternal Revolution

Many people presume that I love babies; after all, that's what I write about, I have witnessed many being born, and have certainly worked with enough newborns in my time, as well as having four children myself. They are usually surprised when I confess that actually I'm not too crazy about them and I'm certainly not clamoring at the front of the queue to hold a newborn.

In fact, I can take or leave a baby, however chubby their cheeks or cute their coos. What I really like are the mothers. I love watching the metamorphosis of a woman from being carefree and childless, growing, in more ways than one, through her pregnancy. I love the whole process of birth and in particular I love the energy that all women muster up in them during their birthing, and how they often seem like some ethereal creature, so strong and yet so delicate.

Most of all I love watching the change in women when their baby arrives. They develop a new softness that they never had before; a new dimension to their personality that is fascinating to watch unfold. Lastly they develop confidence and this is the most magical change of all to watch appear. I will never tire of meeting a nervous new mother unsure of her own abilities, disbelieving in her own instinct, and confused from a myriad of conflicting advice and watching her slowly, gradually, often without her realizing, gaining a little confidence each day. Slowly she blossoms, unfolding like the petals on a rose; many times you can almost see the radiance of confidence around her as she learns to trust herself and her baby.

This is what I like. I love to witness the change from shy and unconfident new mother to one who is happy in her own skin and one who knows she is the best expert when it comes to her own baby. I am honored sometimes to be allowed to play a part in this process, whether it is in the flesh or through the pages of this book.

I don't want to be a "baby expert," largely because I am not one, but also because that would detract from the mothers themselves, for they are the experts—just as you are an expert too, I hope now that you realize that.

This is what we at BabyCalm™ mean when we talk about our "maternal revolution"; we want to help all mothers around the world to go through this process of self-awareness, to trust that they do have a maternal instinct, and to trust that they know best for their own child. Constantly giving a new mother advice is disempowering, so instead we aim to support the mother to find her own way on her journey; in fact we often refer to ourselves as "tour guides" rather than teachers.

For it is only when a mother finds her own way that her inner strength, confidence, and maternal instinct really shines. Remember, too, your role as a mother is to be "good enough," no mother is perfect, and everybody makes mistakes, whatever they may say! And you are just that, good enough. In fact I am certain you are more. Your baby already knows that; your last part of the journey is to learn to believe in yourself!

Resources for New Parents

You may find some of these contacts and resources handy for life with a young baby.

Breastfeeding Support

La Leche League Helpline: (877) 452-5324

National Breastfeeding Helpline: (800) 994-9662

InfantRisk Center (medication during breastfeeding): (806) 352-2519

www.breastfeedingusa.org
Breastfeeding information

www.lllusa.org
La Leche League USA

www.kellymom.com
Kellymom—great breastfeeding information website

www.breastfeedingonline.com
Breastfeeding articles and videos from Dr. Jack Newman

Other Support

www.babycalming.com
For BabyCalm™ classes, workshops, and support near you

www.dona.org
Doulas of North America doula finder and directory

www.babywearingschool.com
Find your local BabyWearing consultant

www.acatoday.org
American Chiropractic Association

www.osteopathic.org
American Osteopathic Association

www.solaceformothers.org
Support for mothers suffering from birth trauma

www.postpartum.net
Support for postnatal depression

www.nomotc.org
For parents of twins and more

www.iaim.net
International Association of Infant Massage

www.babywearinginternational.com
Babywearing help and advice

Recommended Products

All available worldwide from www.babycalming.com:

Humanity Co-sleeper: a special pad and bumper to stop your baby falling out of the parents' bed when bed sharing

BabyCalm™ Mother's Relaxation CD: to smooth your transition into motherhood

BabyCalm™ Baby Calming CD: white noise, to calm your baby and aid sleep

Battery aromatherapy fan: used as a sleep aid in your baby's nursery

BabyCalm™ swaddle sheet: a large square brushed-cotton sheet

Moby wrap sling: a great beginner sling suitable from birth

The World of Creatures: a 100 percent natural and gentle toiletry range for babies

Bibliography

Abernethy, V. *Population Pressure and Cultural Adjustment.* Piscataway, NJ: Transaction Publishers, 2005.

American Academy of Pediatrics. *Caring for Your Baby and Young Child: Birth to Age 5.* New York: Bantam, 1994.

De Benedictis, T., PhD, H. Larson, G. Kemp, MA, S. Barston, and R. Segal, MA. *Understanding Sleep: sleep needs, cycles, and stages.* Helpguide.org, 2007.

Blois, M., MD. *Babywearing: The Benefits and Beauty of This Ancient Tradition.* Amarillo, TX: Pharmasoft Publishing, 2005.

Bucknam, R., and G. Ezzo. *On Becoming Babywise: Giving Your Infant the Gift of Nighttime Sleep.* South Carolina: Parent-Wise Solutions, 1995.

Diamant, A. *The Red Tent.* London: Pan Macmillan, 2002.

Dunstan, P. *Child Sense: How to Speak Your Baby's Language.* London: Hodder & Stoughton, 2010.

Edelman, H. *Motherless Mothers, How Mother Loss Shapes the Parents We Become.* New York: Harper Paperbacks, 2007.

Ferber, R. *Solve Your Child's Sleep Problems.* New York: Simon & Schuster Inc., 1986.

Fleiss, P. *Sweet Dreams: A Pediatrician's Secrets for Your Child's Good Night's Sleep.* Los Angeles: Lowell House, 2000.

Ford, G. *The New Contented Little Baby Book.* London: Vermilion, 2006.

Gerhardt, S. *Why Love Matters—How Affection Shapes a Baby's Brain*. Oxford: Routledge, 2004.

Halfmoon, H. L. *Primal Mothering in a Modern World*. El Cajon, CA: Sunfood Nutrition, 1998.

Hall, T. *Save Our Sleep: Helping Your Baby to Sleep Through the Night*. London: Vermilion, 2010.

Hogg, T. *Secrets of the Baby Whisperer*. London: Vermilion, 2001.

Holt, E. *The Care and Feeding of Children, a Catechism for the Use of Mothers and Children's Nurses*. Unknown, 1895.

Jackson, D. *Three in a Bed: The Benefits of Sleeping with Your Baby* (2nd edition). London: Bloomsbury, 1999.

James, O. *How Not to F Them Up*. London: Vermilion, 2011.

King, T. *Feeding and Care of Baby*. Oxford: Oxford University Press, 1942.

Kitzinger, S. *The Crying Baby*. London: Viking, 1989; republished by Carroll and Brown, 2005.

Konner, M. *Childhood: A Multicultural View*, London: Little, Brown, 1991.

Koudris, M. *The Diary of an Unborn Child*. Berkshire: Gateway, 1992.

Leboyer, F. *Birth Without Violence*. London: Pinter and Martin, 2011.

Liedloff, J. *The Continuum Concept*. London: Penguin, 1989.

Lullaby Trust: www.lullabytrust.org.uk/

McClure, V. *Infant Massage: A Handbook for Loving Parents*. London: Souvenir Press Ltd, 1989.

McKenna, J. *Sleeping with Your Baby, A Parent's Guide to Cosleeping.* Washington, DC: Platypus Media, 2007.

Millan, C. *Be the Pack Leader: Use Cesar's Way to Transform Your Dog . . . and Your Life.* London: Hodder Paperbacks, 2009.

Mohrbacher, N. *Breastfeeding Answer Book.* Schaumburg, IL: La Leche League International, 2003.

Murray, L. *The Social Baby.* Fond du Lac, WI: CP Publishing, 2005.

Odent, M. *Primal Health: Understanding the Critical Period Between Birth and the First Birthday.* West Sussex: Clairview Books, 2007.

Imogen O'Reilly: www.alternative-mama.com.

Royal College of Midwives. *Successful Breastfeeding* (3rd edition). Philadelphia: Churchill Livingstone, 2002.

William Sears: www.askdrsears.com.

Sears, W., and M. Sears, *The Attachment Parenting Book.* London: Little, Brown, 2001.

Stadlen, N. *How Mothers Love.* London: Piatkus, 2011.

—. *What Mothers Do.* London: Piatkus, 2005.

Sunderland, M. *The Science of Parenting.* London: Dorling Kindersley, 2008.

Tantum, J., and B. Want. *Baby Secrets: How to Know Your Baby's Needs.* London: Michael Joseph, 2005.

van de Rijt, H., and F. Plooij. *The Wonder Weeks.* Arnhem, The Netherlands: Kiddy World Promotions, 2010.

Watson, J. B. *Psychological Care of Infant and Child.* New York: W.W. Norton Company, Inc., 1928.

References

1. J. E. Swain, J. P. Lorberbaum, S. Kose, and L. Strathearn, "Brain basis of early parent—infant interactions: psychology, physiology, and in vivo functional neuroimaging studies," *Journal Child Psychology Psychiatry* (April 2007); 48(3–4): 262–87.

2. G. Love, N. Torrey, I. McNamara, M. Morgan, M. Banks, N. W. Hester, E. R. Glasper, A. C. Devries, C. H. Kinsley, and K. G. Lambert, "Maternal experience produces long-lasting behavioural modifications in the rat," *Behav Neurosci* (August 2005); 119(4): 1,084–96.

3. V. K. Iur'ev, "Maternal instinct and the formation of family-oriented attitude in girls—future mothers," *Sov Zdravookhr* (1991); (1): 17–19.

4. S. P. Chauhan, P. M. Lutton, K. J. Bailey, J. P. Guerrieri, and J. C. Morrison, "Intrapartum clinical, sonographic, and parous patients' estimates of newborn birth weight," *Obstet Gynecol* (June 1992); 79(6): 956–8.

5. *Birth* (September 1999).

6. D. Chamberlain, "Babies are conscious," published by www.eheart. com.

7. D. Narvaez, "The emotional foundations of high moral intelligence," *New Dir Child Adolesc Dev* (Fall 2010); (129): 77–94.

8. J. McKenna, "Babies need their mothers beside them," *World Health* (March–April 1996).

9. J. Golding, M. Pembrey, and R. Jones, "ALSPAC—the Avon Longitudinal Study of Parents and Children," *Paediatr Perinat Epidemiol* (January 2001); 15(1): 74–87.

10. Abdulrazzaq, Al Kendi, and Nagelkerke, "Soothing methods used to calm a baby in an Arab country," *Acta Paediatr* (February 2009); 98(2): 392–6.

11. Mitchell, Blair, and L'Hoir, "Dummies. Should pacifiers be recommended to prevent sudden infant death syndrome?," *Pediatrics* (May 2006); 117(5): 1,755–8.

12. R. Y. Moon, K. O. Tanabe, D. C. Yang, H. A. Young, and F. R. Hauck, "Pacifier use and SIDS: evidence for a consistently reduced risk," *Matern Child Health J* (April 20, 2011).

13. Alcantra, "The chiropractic care of infants with colic," International Chiropractic Pediatric Association (June 2011).

14. M. Niemelä, O. Pihakari, T. Pokka, and M. Uhari, "Pacifier as a risk factor for acute otitis media: a randomized, controlled trial of parental counseling," *Pediatrics* (September 2000); 106(3): 483–8.

15. M. M. Rovers, M. E. Numans, E. Langenbach, D. E. Grobbee, T. J. Verheij, and A. G. Schilder, "Is pacifier use a risk factor for acute otitis media? A dynamic cohort study," *Fam Pract* (August 2008); 25(4): 233–6. Epub June 17, 2008.

16. B. Ogaard, E. Larsson, and R. Lindsten, "The effect of sucking habits, cohort, sex, intercanine arch widths, and breast or bottle feeding on posterior crossbit in Norwegian and Swedish 3-year-old children," *Am J Orthod Dentofacial Orthop* (August 1994); 106(2): 161–6.

17. A. T. Gerd, S. Bergman, J. Dahlgren, J. Roswall, and B. Alm, "Factors associated with discontinuation of breastfeeding before 1 month of age," *Acta Paediatr* (January 2012); 101(1): 55–60. doi: 10.1111/j.1651-2227.2011.02405.x. Epub July 22, 2011.

18. S. H. Jaafar, S. Jahanfar, M. Angolkar, and J. J. Ho, "Pacifier use versus no pacifier use in breastfeeding term infants for increasing

duration of breastfeeding," *Cochrane Database Syst Rev* (March 16, 2011); (3):CD007202.

19. J. A. Spencer, D. J. Moran, A. Lee, and D. Talbert, "White noise and sleep induction," *Arch Dis Child* (January 1990); 65(1): 135-7.

20. K. Coleman-Phox, R. Odouli, and D. K. Li, "Use of a fan during sleep and the risk of sudden infant death syndrome," *Arch Pediatr Adolesc Med* (October 2008); 162(10): 963-8.

21. U. A. Hunziker and R. G. Barr, "Increased carrying reduces infant crying: a randomized controlled trial," *Pediatrics* (May 1986); 77(5): 641-8.

22. E. Anisfeld, V. Casper, M. Nozyce, and N. Cunningham, "Does infant carrying promote attachment? An experimental study of the effects of increased physical contact on the development of attachment," *Child Development* (October 1990); 61(5): 1,617-27.

23. A. A. Kane, L. E. Mitchell, K. P. Craven, and J. L. Marsh, "Observations on a recent increase of plagiocephaly without synostosis," *Pediatrics* (1996); 97: 877-85.

24. J. Persing et al., "Prevention and management of positional skull deformities in infants', American Academy of Pediatrics Committee on Practice and Ambulatory Medicine, Section on Plastic Surgery and Section on Neurological Surgery," *Pediatrics* (July 2003); 112 (1): 199-202.

25. J. S. Lonstein, "Regulation of anxiety during the postpartum period," *Frontiers in Neuroendocrinology* (September 2007); 28: 2-3.

26. K. L. Armstrong, R. A. Quinn, and M. R. Dadds, "The sleep patterns of normal children," *Med J Australia* (194); 1:161(3): 202-6.

27. H. L. Ball, "Breastfeeding, bed-sharing, and infant sleep," *Birth* (2003); 30(3): 181-8.

28. A. Scher, "A longitudinal study of night waking in the first year," *Child Care Health Dev* (September–October 1991); 17(5): 295–302.

29. J. Golding, M. Pembrey, and R. Jones, "ALSPAC—the Avon Longitudinal Study of Parents and Children," *Paediatr Perinat Epidemiol* (January 2001); 15(1): 74–87.

30. K. L. Armstrong, R. A. Quinn, and M. R. Dadds, "The sleep patterns of normal children," *Med J Australia* (1994); 1:161(3): 202–6.

31. J. Golding, M. Pembrey, and R. Jones, "ALSPAC—the Avon Longitudinal Study of Parents and Children," *Paediatr Perinat Epidemiol* (January 2001); 15(1): 74–87.

32. D. Blunt Bugental et al., "The hormonal costs of subtle forms of infant maltreatment", *Hormones and Behaviour* (January 2003); 237–44.

33. J. D. Bremmer et al., "The effects of stress on memory and the hippocampus throughout the life cycle: implications for childhood development and aging," *Developmental Psychology* (1998); 10: 871–85.

34. G. Dawson et al., "The role of early experience in shaping behavioral and brain development and its implications for social policy," *Development and Psychopathology* (2000); 12(4): 695–712.

35. J. P. Henry and S. Wang, "Effects of early stress on adult affiliative behavior," *Psychoneuroendocrinology* (1998); 23(8): 863–75.

36. T. Doan, A. Gardiner, C. L. Gay, et al., "Breast-feeding increases sleep duration of new parents," *J Perinat Neonatal Nurs* (2007); 21(3): 200–6.

37. D. Blunt Bugental et al., "The hormonal costs of subtle forms of infant maltreatment," *Hormones and Behaviour* (January 2003); 237–44.

38. J. D. Bremmer et al., "The effects of stress on memory and the hippocampus throughout the life cycle: implications for childhood development and aging," *Developmental Psychology* (1998); 10: 871–85.

39. G. Dawson et al., "The role of early experience in shaping behavioral and brain development and its implications for social policy," *Development and Psychopathology* (2000); 12(4): 695–712.

40. J. P. Henry and S. Wang, "Effects of early stress on adult affiliative behavior," *Psychoneuroendocrinology* (1998); 23(8): 863–75.

41. K. D. Ramos and D. M. Youngclarke, "Parenting advice books about child sleep: cosleeping and crying it out," *Sleep* (December 2006); 29(12): 1,616–23.

42. W. Middlemiss, D. A. Granger, W. A. Goldberg, and L. Nathans, "Asynchrony of mother–infant–hypothalamic–pituitary–adrenal axis activity following extinction of infant crying responses induced during the transition to sleep." *Early Hum Dev* (September 22, 2011).

43. K. D. Ramos and D. M. Youngclarke, "Parenting advice books about child sleep: cosleeping and crying it out," *Sleep* (December 2006); 29(12): 1,616–23.

44. S. L. Blunden, K. R. Thompson, and D. Dawson, "Behavioural sleep treatments and night time crying in infants: challenging the status quo," *Sleep Med Rev* (October 2011); 15(5): 327–34.

45. W. Middlemiss, D. A. Granger, W. A. Goldberg, and L. Nathans, "Asynchrony of mother–infant–hypothalamic–pituitary–adrenal axis activity following extinction of infant crying responses induced during the transition to sleep," *Early Hum Dev* (September 22, 2011).

46. J. P. Olives, "When should we introduce gluten into the feeding of the new-born babies?," *Arch Pediatr* (December 2010);17 Suppl 5: S199–203.

47. O. Hernell, A. Ivarsson, and L. A. Persson, "Coeliac disease: effect of early feeding on the incidence of the disease," *Early Hum Dev* (November 2001); 65 Suppl:S 153–60.

48. S. Halken, "Prevention of allergic disease in childhood: clinical and epidemiological aspects of primary and secondary allergy prevention," *Pediatr Allery Immunol* (June 2004); 15 Suppl 16: 4–5, 9–32.

49. H. Y. Dong and W. Wang, "Clinical observations on curative effect of TCM massage on dyssomnia of infants," *J Tradit Chin Med* (December 2010); 30(4): 299–301.

50. W. A. Hall, M. Clauson, E. M. Carty, P. A. Janssen, and R. A. Saunders, "Effects on parents of an intervention to resolve infant behavioral sleep problems," *Pediatr Nurs* (May–June 2006); 32(3): 243–9.

51. A. Kulkarni, J. S. Kaushik, P. Gupta, H. Sharma, and R. K. Agrawal, "Massage and touch therapy in neonates: the current evidence," *Indian Pediatr* (September 2010); 47(9): 771–6.

52. Mechtild, Vennemann, H.-W. Hense, T. Bajanowski, Blair, C. Complojer, R. Y. Moon, and U. Kiechl-Kohlendorfer, "Bed sharing and the risk of sudden infant death syndrome: can we resolve the debate?," *J Pediatr* (January 2012); 160(1): 44–48.e2. Epub August 24, 2011.

53. H. L. Ball, E. Moya, L. Fairley, J. Westman, S. Oddie, and J. Wright, "Infant care practices related to sudden infant death syndrome in South Asian and white British families in the UK," *Paediatr Perinat Epidemiol* (January 2012); 26(1): 3–12. doi: 10.1111/j.1365-3016.2011.01217.x. Epub August 18, 2011.

54. S. Mosko, C. Richard, and J. McKenna, "Infant arousals during mother–infant bed sharing: implications for infant sleep and sudden infant death syndrome research," *Pediatrics* (1997); 100: 841–9.

55. J. McKenna, "Babies need their mothers beside them," *World Health* (March–April 1996).

56. B. E. Morgan, A. R. Horn, and N. J. Bergman, "Should neonates sleep alone?," *Biol Psychiatry* (November 1, 2011); 70(9): 817–25. Epub July 29, 2011.

57. J. McKenna, "Babies need their mothers beside them," *World Health* (March–April 1996).

58. S. Mosko, C. Richard, and J. McKenna, "Infant arousals during mother–infant bed sharing: implications for infant sleep and sudden infant death syndrome research," *Pediatrics* (1997); 100: 841–9.

59. B. E. Morgan, A. R. Horn, and N. J. Bergman, "Should neonates sleep alone?," *Biol Psychiatry* (November 1, 2011); 70(9): 817–25. Epub July 29, 2011.

60. J. J. McKenna, "Cultural influences on infant and childhood sleep biology, and the science that studies it: toward a more inclusive paradigm." In: J. Loughlin, J. Carroll, and C. Marcus, editors, *Sleep and Breathing in Children: a developmental approach,* Marcell Dakker (2000), pp. 199–230.

61. W. Middlemiss, D. A. Granger, W. A. Goldberg, and L. Nathans, "Asynchrony of mother–infant–hypothalamic–pituitary–adrenal axis activity following extinction of infant crying responses induced during the transition to sleep," *Early Hum Dev* (September 22, 2011).

62. B. E. Morgan, A. R. Horn, and N. J. Bergman, "Should neonates sleep alone?," *Biol Psychiatry* (November 1, 2011); 70(9): 817–25. Epub July 29, 2011.

63. W. S. Rholes, J. A. Simpson, J. L. Kohn, C. L. Wilson, A. M. Martin III, S. Tran, and D. A. Kashy, "Attachment orientations and depression: a longitudinal study of new parents," *J Pers Soc Psychol* (April 2011); 100(4): 567–86.

64. F. Pedrosa Gil and R. Rupprecht, "Current aspects of attachment theory and development psychology as well as neurobiological aspects in psychiatric and psychosomatic disorders," *Nervenarzt* (November 2003); 74(11): 965–71.

65. D. Narvaez, "The emotional foundations of high moral intelligence," *New Dir Child Adolesc Dev*, (Fall 2010); (129): 77–94.

66. N. Franc, M. Maury, and D. Purper-Ouakil, "ADHD and attachment processes: are they related?," *Encephale* (June 2009); 35(3): 256–61. Epub September 20, 2008.

67. R. L. Scott and J. V. Cordova, "The influence of adult attachment styles on the association between marital adjustment and depressive symptoms," *J Fam Psychol* (June 2002); 16(2): 199–208.

68. M. Rutter, "Clinical implications of attachment concepts: retrospect and prospect," *J Child Psychol Psychiatry* (May 1995); 36(4): 549–71.

69. M. M. Oriña, W. A. Collins, J. A. Simpson, J. E. Salvatore, K. C. Haydon, and J. S. Kim, "Developmental and dyadic perspectives on commitment in adult romantic relationships," *Psychol Sci* (July 2011); 22(7): 908–15. Epub May 26, 2011.

70. D. Narvaez, "Dangers of 'Crying it out': damaging children and their relationships for the longterm," *Psychology Today* (December 2011).

71. M. M. Oriña, W. A. Collins, J. A. Simpson, J. E. Salvatore, K. C. Haydon, and J. S. Kim, "Developmental and dyadic perspectives on commitment in adult romantic relationships," *Psychol Sci* (July 2011); 22(7): 908–15. Epub May 26, 2011.

72. L. M. Gartner, J. Morton, R. A. Lawrence, A. J. Naylor, D. O'Hare, R. J. Schanler, and A. I. Eidelman, "American Academy of Pediatrics Section on Breastfeeding. Breastfeeding and the use of human milk," *Pediatrics* (February 2005); 115(2): 496–506.

73. M. A. Wessel et al., "Paroxysmal fussing in infancy, sometimes called 'colic'," *Pediatrics* (1954); 14: 421–43.

74. P. Rautava, H. Helenius, and L. Lehtonen, "Psychosocial predisposing factors for infantile colic," *BMJ* (1993); 307: 600–4.

75. I. Jakobsson and T. Lindberg, "Cows' milk proteins cause infantile colic in breastfed infants: a double blind crossover study," *Pediatrics* (1983); 71: 268.

76. K. D. Lust, J. E. Brown, and W. Thomas, "Maternal intake of cruciferous vegetables and other food, and colic symptoms in exclusively breast-fed infants," *J Am Diet Assoc* (1996); 96(1): 46–8.

77. D. J. Moore, D. Dreckow, T. A. Robb, and G. P. Davidson, "Breath H2 and behavioural response in breast and formula fed infants with colic to modified lactose intake," *J Paediatr and Child Health* (1991); 27: 128.

78. M. M. Garrison and D. A. Christakis, "A systematic review of treatments for infant colic," *Pediatrics* (July 2000); 106(1 Pt 2): 184–90.

79. J. Headley and K. Northstone, "Medication administered to children from 0 to 7.5 years in the Avon Longitudinal Study of Parents and Children (ALSPAC)," *Eur J Clin Pharmacol* (February 2007); 63(2): 189–95. Epub January 3, 2007.

80. J. Critch, "Infantile colic: is there a role for dietary interventions?," *Paediatr Child Health* (January 2011); 16(1): 47–9.

81. P. M. Sherman, E. Hassall, U. Fagundes-Neto, B. D. Gold, S. Kato, S. Koletzko, S. Orenstein, C. Rudolph, N. Vakil, and Y. Vandenplas, "A global, evidence-based consensus on the definition of gastroesophageal reflux disease in the pediatric population," *Arch Pediatr* (November 2010); 17(11): 1,586–93. Epub October 12, 2010.

Index

Note: page numbers in **bold** refer to diagrams